Anonymous

Education in Alaska

Anonymous

Education in Alaska

ISBN/EAN: 9783337817770

Printed in Europe, USA, Canada, Australia, Japan

Cover: Foto ©ninafisch / pixelio.de

More available books at **www.hansebooks.com**

[*Whole Number 246.*

UNITED STATES BUREAU OF EDUCATION.

REPRINT OF CHAPTER XXXV OF THE REPORT OF THE COMMISSIONER
OF EDUCATION FOR 1896-97, WITH INTRODUCTORY STATEMENT
BY THE COMMISSIONER OF EDUCATION.

EDUCATION IN ALASKA

1896-97.

SHELDON JACKSON, LL. D.,
GENERAL AGENT.

WASHINGTON:
GOVERNMENT PRINTING OFFICE.
1898.

FROM THE

INTRODUCTORY STATEMENT

OF THE

COMMISSIONER OF EDUCATION

FOR THE

REPORT OF 1896-97.

Education in Alaska.—During the past two years by reason of the numerous discoveries of gold in Alaska that Territory has become an object of great interest. A school established at Circle City, on the upper Yukon, near the boundary between United States and British America, had a successful session during its first year, but on account of the removal of the inhabitants from Circle City to the region of the Klondike has lost nearly all of its pupils and has been closed for the present year. Large numbers of immigrants collected with their families at Dyea and Skagway seemed to demand accommodations for their children in school, but the present state of rapid change, not only of routes but of mining localities at the ends of those routes, makes it uncertain whether a school established for the children of the families of miners could have a longer term of existence than the one at Circle City, which seemed two years ago likely to become a permanent center for mining operations.

The missionaries representing the great bodies of Christian faith have thus far selected what may be called the strategical points for influence upon the native population of Alaska.

From the beginning, in 1885-86 on to 1893-94, it had been the policy of the Bureau of Education to subsidize mission schools in all places where it was not possible to establish Government day schools. The population of Indian villages is more or less nomadic, summering in camps on the seas and rivers at good fishing places, and wintering in their villages, located in more sheltered situations. The arrival of white immigrants has given a fixed character to these villages, in the southeast part of Alaska especially. In the southeastern region, in the presence of a larger or smaller contingent of white population, it has been found possible to establish Government schools and organize local school committees to supervise them. But in northern and western Alaska, villages with a nucleus of white population are not to be found, except at the ports of Unalaska and St. Michael; and in order to reach the natives successfully, it is necessary to avail one's self of the mission stations, 3 of which are located on the Arctic Ocean, 9 on the Bering Sea, and 7 in the river valley of the Yukon, making a total of 19 missions with 61 missionaries. These mission stations have been located, in the light of a great deal of experience, at such places as furnish natural centers for the native population and at the same time afford the best facilities for communication with the United States in the short summer season. For the long winter season of eight to nine months no communication has been possible hitherto with northwestern Alaska.

In subsidizing the mission schools a certain minimum of school enrollment has been required, and a certain sum per pupil allowed, not to exceed in the aggregate a fixed sum agreed upon. The example of the Indian Bureau has been closely followed in this matter, except that where the Indian Bureau has allowed subsidies of $167 per annum this Bureau has allowed from $90 to $150 per pupil, boarded, clothed, and instructed, and $30 for day pupils. The maximum amount paid to contract schools appears in the year 1889–90, when the sum of $31,174.12 was paid. The largest item of that year was paid for industrial instruction and apparatus necessary to facilitate the same. In the year 1892–93 the action of Congress with regard to the Indian Bureau in the matter of contract schools was taken as indicating a policy to withdraw appropriations from contract schools, and for that reason the amount paid to contract schools in that year was reduced from $28,980 to $17,040—almost 40 per cent, and in 1893–94 it was further reduced to $8,000. In the year 1894–95 the subsidizing of contract schools was entirely discontinued, but in a few cases Government teachers were assigned to the mission stations.

The mission stations not only have the advantage of being located in important centers of the native population in the north and west, but they bring with them certain other advantages which the Government may use for its purposes of instructing the natives in the English language and in the arts of civilized life. In the first place, the mission station is a very effective center for the spread of the use of the English language among the natives, educating not only the children who come to its schools, but also the adult population attending its religious services or coming into any business relation with it whatever. I have already mentioned that there are 19 missionary centers and a corps of 61 missionaries in northwestern and central Alaska extending daily this educational influence to entire communities of Indians or Eskimos.

In 1885 General Eaton, as Commissioner of Education, secured the services of Dr. Sheldon Jackson as general agent for education in Alaska, which had recently been placed under the charge of the Secretary of the Interior. Dr. Jackson had been appointed superintendent of home missions for several States and Territories in the Northwest as early as 1869, and had distinguished himself by the vigor with which he extended the work in the far west. In 1870 he took charge of the work of home missions in the vast region from Mexico to Canada and from Nevada to Nebraska. In the early days before railroads had penetrated those regions he traveled on foot or used ox carts or mustang ponies. In the prosecution of his work he traveled in thirteen years 345,027 miles, or an average of 26,540 miles a year. He established and for ten years conducted the "Rocky Mountain Presbyterian." In 1877 he visited Alaska as the first ordained missionary from the United States, and in the next eight years he rapidly established schools and churches in the archipelago, and commenced the process of civilization which has gone on in Alaska ever since. In 1880 he built the church and founded the Industrial Training School for native children at Sitka.

After his appointment as United States agent his trips to the northwest were undertaken for the most part in the *Bear*, a revenue cutter sent out annually by the Secretary of the Treasury. Its captain (M. A. Healy) interested himself warmly in the cause represented by Dr. Jackson in this region, and to him is due in a measure the success in establishing schools in northwest Alaska. And to him and Dr. Jackson is due the original suggestion of the plan of stocking the enormous moss fields of Alaska with herds of reindeer and the training of the natives into skilled herdsmen and teamsters.

It had been obvious, from the beginning of the Government subsidies in 1885-86, that there should be not only education in elementary English branches, but also a training in the employments of civilized life. From the first, at all the missions there was instruction in cooking, housekeeping, and clothes making. Then followed more careful education in the trades of carpentering, blacksmithing, and shoemaking, subsidizing for this instruction the Presbyterian Industrial School at Sitka. As early as 1891 the matter of the introduction of reindeer into Alaska had been brought to my attention by Dr. Sheldon Jackson and Captain Healy, of the United States revenue cutter *Bear*. Upon learning that tame reindeer could be obtained from points in Siberia opposite to Alaska, and that all of Alaska (excepting the river valleys and places on the coast covered with forests) bore large quantities of the kind of moss that furnishes the best food for the reindeer, I became so much interested in the project of introducing the reindeer into northwestern Alaska that I urged Dr. Jackson to appeal to the friends of missionary education for a preliminary sum to begin the experiment at once. From the sum of $2,156 thus procured a first purchase of 16 deer was made in the summer of 1891, and a herd of 171 in the summer of 1892. The Government appropriation of $6,000 became available for the support of reindeer in the summer of 1893, and a further purchase of 124 deer was made, and for the summer of 1894 a still further purchase of 123 was made out of an appropriation of $7,500, making a total of 538 deer purchased in Siberia and placed in a Government herd near Port Clarence. The 16 deer purchased in 1891 have been

REINDEER RIDER IN EASTERN SIBERIA.
By W. H. Jackson.

allowed to run wild on one of the eastern Aleutian Islands, and since then have in a measure stocked that island with reindeer. From this original herd of 538 reindeer a total number of 1,323 fawns have been born, making an aggregate of 1,861, of which 395 have been lost, injured, or killed in various ways during the five years, leaving 1,466 reindeer in the herds August, 1897.

A plan has been gradually matured for the use of these reindeer in the scheme of education. Two objects are to be secured: (1) The training of the natives as herders and as teamsters. This implies that the natives must be interested in the project; they must take the long step from nomadic fishermen and hunters to dwellers in villages, with permanent employments that will support them and also render them useful to a white population which will eventually come to central and northwestern Alaska. (2) The other important object to be gained is the education of these natives in thrift, so that they will preserve and accumulate the reindeer intrusted to them.

At each mission station there is constantly going on a process of selecting the trustworthy natives—those ambitious to learn the civilization of the white men, those ambitious to hold and increase property. Reindeer intrusted to the ordinary individual savage would disappear within twelve months after the gift.

At the reindeer station a number of apprentices have been selected and rewards for intelligent and persevering industry offered. They were to receive two reindeer for the first year's apprenticeship; at the end of the second year five more, in such a way as to gradually develop the sense of individual ownership of property—a sense which has never been developed in the tribal relation.

[From letter of instruction by Dr. Jackson to the superintendent of the reindeer herd.]

PORT CLARENCE,
UNITED STATES REVENUE-MARINE STEAMER BEAR,
July 4, 1893.

SIR: * * * The herders are to be fed and clothed and housed, also furnished with tobacco or its equivalent, at Government expense. The Siberian herders and the experienced Eskimo, each one will receive, in addition to the above, $50 worth of barter goods at the end of the year and the inexperienced ones $30 worth. If they prefer it they can be paid a portion of the above from time to time as they may need it, only that at the end of the year the amount received shall not exceed the total amount allowed.

When food is plenty and cheap you will purchase with the supplies at the station such oil, meat, dried fish, skins, etc., as are needed at the station. You are also authorized to purchase wood from the natives.

In addition to the paid herders, it is desired that you take into the station a number of wide-awake young men to learn the management of deer. They will be fed, clothed, and housed at Government expense. If they have been faithful to their duties and have shown aptitude in learning for one full year at the station you are authorized to allow them two deer, which can be marked with their brand, but must be continued in the general herd. At the end of the second year you can give them five more. I think it will be well to encourage them to remain with the herd for three or four years, when they will have sufficient deer, so that two or three of the herders, by combining their holdings, can start a new herd.

If, after a fair trial of a few months, a young man is lazy, indifferent, or dull, you had better send him away from the station and give his place to a more promising one. There is a constant sifting process going on among white men, and the same process is equally needful among the natives.

I would like the first herders especially to be picked men—the ablest and best among their people—as that class will alone secure the best results from the introduction of the deer.

Under the regulations established 9 apprentices have received reindeer—from 2 to 7 each. The total number of reindeer originally assigned to them being 52, the same had increased last August by the birth of fawns to 133.

From the beginning, schoolbooks and apparatus have been furnished for the schools in Alaska. Reindeer are the schoolbooks and apparatus necessary for the education of the western and northern natives. To secure the chief object aimed at in the importation of reindeer from Siberia, it is evident that the reindeer must eventually come into the hands of thrifty persons among the natives, who will preserve the herds, increase them, break them to harness, and make them available, under the management of trained teamsters, for the use of white immigrants who settle in Alaska. The missionary stations furnish the only safe centers for the location of herds and the establishment of schools of instruction in the rearing of the reindeer and in the training of them to harness.

As already mentioned, the missions ascertain the capable and teachable youth among the natives. They are able at any time to furnish a list of the natives in their vicinities noted for good character. At each of these stations 20 or 30 youth, selected from a village population of 300 or more, can be put in training as herdsmen and teamsters. No matter how large the Government appropriation should be, therefore, it would be necessary to connect the reindeer instruction and the establishment of permanent herds in northwest Alaska with these missionary stations.

The small herds loaned to each missionary station as a Government aid are in the nature of an outfit of industrial apparatus. The report of the Indian Bureau shows that the United States Government furnished 10,000 head of stock for the period of 1890–96 for one Indian agency (the Blackfeet), and that seeds, implements, stock, wagons, harness, in large amounts, have been furnished to other agencies. These donations are certainly more justifiable than donations made to prevent the savage peoples from starving, for they are given in the form of apparatus for the instruction of these peoples in the industrial arts and in the practice of thrift. All these things prevent starvation. Just as in the agricultural colleges of the several States the Government money is used to pay for the stock of the model farm, which is used as the apparatus for the instruction of the pupils, so the reindeer herd is used as apparatus loaned to the missionary stations for the purpose of instruction of the natives. But from three to five years' apprenticeship is needed for the full training of apprentices in the management of reindeer.

Persons who have been brought up to the care of neat cattle and horses, or sheep only, have not thereby acquired the art of managing reindeer, for this requires special apprenticeship. With the first herd (that of 1892) Siberian herdsmen were procured to give instruction in these arts, but the degree of success was so small that in 1894 five families of Laplanders were obtained to take their place. The Laplanders, being a civilized people and devoid of the superstitions which embarrass the Siberian natives, have attained a higher degree of skill in the management of this animal, and also show greater ability in teaching others what they know. After obtaining the reindeer, therefore, the next important matter is the procurement of skilled herdsmen and teamsters from Norway and Sweden. It is of little use to give a herd of reindeer to a missionary station unless a skilled teacher goes with it.

The furnishing of the properly trained Laplander is one of the chief items of expense in the introduction of reindeer into northwestern Alaska. A salary of $200 to $500 a year is necessary for each, and the distribution of the herd at the different points on the seacoast and in the interior is possible only in so far as the Government is able to send these experienced herdsmen and teamsters. In the course of eight or ten years there will grow up a supply of thoroughly educated natives who will render it unnecessary to depend any longer upon Lapland and Finland for teachers. But it is hoped in the meanwhile that there will be some migration from Scandinavia of families of herdsmen and teamsters.

Thus far the original plan of distributing small herds to the missionary stations and furnishing teachers to care for the herds has been put into operation in only four instances. To the missionary station at Cape Prince of Wales, nearest to the Teller Station at Port Clarence, 118 deer were furnished in August, 1894, and Mr. Lopp, who had mastered the art of caring for the reindeer, having been with our herd from the beginning, was made the Government teacher and paid a salary.

The following year 112 deer were loaned to the most promising apprentice, Anti-sarlook (called Charlie), stationed at Cape Nome. In 1896 two other herds of 50 each were loaned, respectively, to the Swedish Evangelical Mission on Golovin Bay and the Episcopal Mission at Fort Adams, on the middle Yukon, near the mouth of the Tanana River. These herds have been loaned on the condition that they are used as apparatus for the instruction of natives in the art of herding deer and training them to harness, and on condition that after three years the Government may take from the herd a number of deer in good condition equal to the original number furnished, the stations retaining the increase. And, pursuing this policy, negotiations have been for some time in progress to loan herds on the same conditions to the Catholic stations at Nulato and Koserefski (important places on the Yukon) and also to the stations at Point Hope (Episcopal) and Point Barrow (Presbyterian) on the Arctic Sea; also to the Moravian stations at Bethel, on the Kuskokwim River, and Carmel, on Bristol Bay, at the entrance to the Bering Sea on the south.

In providing education for Alaska it is important that the centers of industrial education shall coincide with the points that have to be held in hand by the Government for the purposes of relief expeditions, and also with those points from which the mining and other industrial interests of Alaska can be governed. To illustrate this I mention the fact that if the herds which it is proposed to establish at Point Barrow and Point Hope, on the Arctic Ocean, can by any means be increased to the number of 5,000 deer, a number not unusual in Lapland as the possession of a single herdsman, the annual increase of such a herd would amount to nearly 2,000 fawns. It is obvious that with such resources at two points on the Arctic there never need be any further fear of starvation on the part of the crews of whaling vessels detained by ice in that region. A saving of at least $50,000 to the Government would have been effected during the year 1897–98 had those herds been in position. Again, had herds of 5,000 each been at the important strategical points of Nulato, on the great bend of the Yukon, at Fort Adams, in the middle Yukon, at the mouth of Tanana River, or at Circle City, on the upper Yukon, the danger to starving miners would have been very much reduced, if not entirely removed.

Communication with Alaska.—The difficulty met with by all those who would visit Alaska is the impossibility of traversing its vast distances in the winter. This is the great obstacle to the miner who wishes to have access to the gold-bearing regions and to carry with him all the conveniences for procuring comfort in the long arctic night. He wishes also to be in constant communication with the friends he has left behind him in the States. This is also the great obstacle to the missionary who wishes to reach the tribes of native population, convert them to Christianity and lead them to adopt the arts of civilized life.

Looking at the map of Alaska, one sees that the great Yukon River penetrates the interior from the west, forming a sort of backbone to the country. Not realizing the climatic conditions, one would suppose that steamboats could keep up for a large portion of the year a communication with the upper branches of that river situated in British America and in the eastern part of Alaska. When he comes to learn, however, that the Yukon River is closed by ice for three-fourths of the year, he looks southward for other avenues to the interior and first notices the inlets of the Northern Pacific between Sitka and

Unalaska, namely, Prince William Sound, Cooks Inlet, and Copper River. But he finds first high mountains and then a vast table-land extending to the north of these places and separating by a distance of from 500 to 700 miles the mining regions of the upper Yukon from the shipping ports on the ocean. These table-lands can not be traversed in the winter by horses or oxen and scarcely even by the hardy species of dogs that are used for transportation in this region. When one considers the difficulties of a journey of 500 to 700 miles through a region without settlements and without stores of provisions, one looks for another approach to the region, namely, to that from the southeast. Bays, or rivers flowing into the archipelago, at the southeast will bring the traveler to the foot of the mountains; then if a good pass may be found that can be used winter and summer, or if its difficulties can be overcome by means of railroads or some method of rapid transportation, the visitor to the interior may find himself at the head waters of the Yukon. In the future of this Territory it is evident that settlements will be formed at distances from 100 to 300 miles apart from the head waters to the mouth of the river. The natural entrance, therefore, into this region in the winter time would appear to be the gateways at the southeast, at the northern extremities of Lynn Sound, or perhaps at Yakutat Bay. This question of communication with Alaska is so important that it deserves a fuller discussion.

I. *The approach to Alaska by way of Bering Sea inadequate for purposes of the Government.*—Vessels that pass into Bering Sea stop at the island of Unalaska, where a village of about 300 people is situated, which contains a Russian church and a Methodist mission. On an island in this harbor, too, the first reindeer, 16 in number, obtained in 1891 for the purpose of introducing the reindeer culture into the schools of northwest Alaska, were turned loose and have increased to a considerable herd, but are running wild on the island.

It has not been possible in ordinary winters to continue the voyage beyond Unalaska (which is the eastern link of the chain known as the Aleutian Islands) into the Bering Sea beyond the Pribyloff Islands in winter. On one occasion, however, St. Matthews Island, 400 miles north of the Pribyloff and about 200 miles south by west of St. Lawrence Island and 400 miles from Bering Strait, was reached, but no vessels have ever been able to land at St. Michael or approach the mouth of the Yukon or any of the bays north or south of this region within a radius of from 50 to 100 miles from the mainland on account of the ice. The ice closes in these ports as early as November 1, and they are not open again until the 15th of June and occasionally (as in 1896) not until the middle of July. These northwestern ports are therefore closed to the Government and to commerce from seven and one-half to eight and one-half months in the year, leaving from three and one-half to four and one-half months for the entire season's work in the northwest.

II. *The approach to the interior of Alaska by way of the inlets of the ocean between Sitka and Unalaska.*—The management of interior Alaska could not be conducted by Bering Sea. But it might be conducted either from some one of the ports on Prince William Sound, or Copper River, which empties next to it on the east, or from Cooks Inlet to the west of it. Some of the streams flowing into these inlets rise near the headwaters of the Tanana, the Forty-Mile Creek, and the White River—the Tanana flowing into the middle Yukon, the Forty-Mile Creek flowing into the Yukon near the place where the Yukon crosses the boundary line that separates Alaska from the British possessions, and the White River flowing into the Yukon some 50 miles above Dawson in British territory. Should a transportation company build a railroad over this route it would furnish a short and ready communication from the south immediately into the river valleys that are rich in gold, and large villages would grow up very soon at the harbor which formed the starting point of the railroad and at its junction and termini. This route would have the advantage of being wholly within the boundaries of Alaska. On this line, at the headwaters of the four rivers mentioned, one branch could go down the Tanana River to Minook on the middle Yukon, and the other branch might approach the upper Yukon with a terminus at or about Circle City or some point farther south, nearer the British boundary and the gold mines of the Klondike. Should this railroad not be built by private parties, an express and mail route could be established by reindeer with relay houses built on the entire route at intervals of from 10 to 20 miles, stocked with provisions and each guarded by one or two soldiers. But the reindeer route could not follow the canyons of the rivers nor extend into the wooded regions near the ocean, because of the lack of moss. The general rule is that where trees grow the moss is not to be found. The moss feeds directly on the rocks until a humus or soil is formed, and then trees begin to grow. Where there is plenty of moisture, as in the river valleys and the coast region, the moss has already given place to trees.

The distance from the southern harbor to the head waters is about 250 miles, and thence to Minook, at the junction of the Tanana and Yukon rivers, is about 300 miles, and about the same distance to the Yukon on the east. Over a good trail in the moss-covered district the reindeer team with the mail could travel at the rate of 100 to 200 miles in the twenty-four hours if relays are furnished once in 50 miles. For in the arctic night one part of the twenty-four hours is as good as another for making a journey. Consequently the mail from the upper Yukon, and all points down to the middle Yukon, could reach, as before asserted, the ocean steamer at Prince William Sound in six days from Minook, and in eight days more would reach Seattle, making communication from all the upper parts of the Yukon two weeks old on reaching Seattle.

Another point of importance is that all of northwest Alaska can be reached by reindeer express from Minook, near the mouth of the Tanana on the middle Yukon. The distance from Minook to St. Michael is about 600 miles, and from Minook to Cape Prince of Wales about 800 miles. It is evident that with reindeer all the way, or with a railroad for a part of the way from Prince William Sound, all parts of Alaska can be reached by reindeer transportation at any time in the winter, and with 50-mile relays the reindeer could bring mail from St. Michael to Minook in six days, and in eight days all the way from Cape Prince of Wales to Minook, or even from Point Barrow, which is the same distance from Minook as the Cape Prince of Wales. Commercial companies could then hear from their whaling fleets, getting news not more than a month old on arrival at Seattle.

III. *The approach to the interior of Alaska by Chilkat on the southeast.*—Southeastern Alaska, including the Alexander Archipelago, in which Sitka and the neighboring islands are situated, is accessible at all times of the year. A bimonthly steamer has for years sailed from Seattle to the northernmost inlet which opens beyond Juneau and extends to Dyea. Since the gold excitement trips are more frequent. Of the harbors in the north of this inlet up Lynn Sound, those at Chilkat and Haines, are deep; that of Dyea is shallow.

Inasmuch as the matter of opening up a railroad communication from Prince William Sound or from Cooks Inlet is a mere project, and inasmuch as it would not be feasible to make a reindeer route to or from either of these places until oceanic steamship lines, or an extension of the steamship line from Sitka has made terminal points of these places, the only alternative for the present action is to complete communication from Chilkat or Haines in the northern inlets of the headwaters of the channel with the upper Yukon by White Pass (from Skagway), Chilkoot Pass (from Dyea), or by Chilkat Pass at the headwaters of the Chilkat River to Lake Arkell, or farther to the west on a route sometimes called the "Dalton trail," a Mr. Dalton having the past season driven some 500 head of cattle and 6,000 sheep over this route to the gold regions. If a railroad should be constructed from Dyea to the navigable waters that descend into the Yukon, there would still be occasion for reindeer transportation 400 or 500 miles beyond to the gold regions for seven or eights months in the year.

The winter climate of Alaska.—It is very difficult to realize the conditions prevalent in Alaska in the winter time. In places where the wind from the southwest comes laden with moisture from the ocean, the snow sometimes falls in the course of the winter to a depth of 12 feet. Where the high mountains cause the south winds to lose a large portion of their moisture the snow fall is much less. The temperature in some months of the year will average many degrees below zero, frequently dipping as low as 50, 60, or even 70 degrees below zero, Fahrenheit. Other months of the same winter will have a temperature, for the entire month, of from zero to freezing point, comparatively comfortable weather. The meteorological records kept in this region show that the coldest month may be December, January, or February. There is great variation from one year to another. Sometimes there is a month in which a storm occurs on an average twice a week for a whole month together. In order to imagine the terrors of a storm in Alaska, one must conceive a perpetual night varying from twilight at midday to the blackest darkness for three-fourths of the day, and in this night he must conceive a Minnesota blizzard in which the thermometer instead of varying from zero to 30 degrees below, as in Minnesota, varies from 30 to 60 degrees below. The impossibility of combating such a storm is obvious.

Communication over the surface of the snow.—For eight months of the year central and northern Alaska may be conceived as a vast snow field; it is not the more difficult to penetrate on that account, however. The snow covers the region like a vast white asphalt pavement. It fills up the small crevices and the deep gulches and makes one smooth surface undulating with the hills and valleys. On the surface of the snow is a hard crust which will bear up men and animals and especially the reindeer with his broad foot. While the winter time can not be used at all for transportation on the Arctic Ocean or Bering Sea or on the rivers of Alaska, the long winter is capable of being used by the reindeer for communication throughout the interior. On a snow surface, with not too steep hills or too deep valleys, the reindeer can travel his 50, 70, or even 90 miles a day, getting his food at meal times by thrusting his tough lips through the snow to the moss.

The supply of reindeer moss for food.—Conceive all Alaska as one vast rock. The forces of nature—the sun, the rains, the frosts, the vital power of the seeds of the moss and of hardy trees—all these elements work on the rock to subdue it for vegetation. On the coast near the ocean where the winds are laden with moisture as well as on the river valleys the first beginnings of vegetation appeared. The rock was eaten into by the moss plant. After the moss had flourished for untold ages it had created a humus or soil in which the seeds of other plants could take root. The moss epoch then was followed by the tree epoch. When the trees grew in the river valleys and on the coast regions the moss could not any longer flourish. But by this time the moss had conquered the rock regions far up the mountain sides and over all the hills in Alaska even up to the Arctic Ocean. This gives at one glance the actual view of the situation in Alaska. Around the southern coasts and in the river valleys trees flourish and moss is not found. Back on the hills and for a mile up the high mountains reindeer moss is to be found in immense quantities. A careful estimate finds sufficient food for ten millions of reindeer, basing the estimate on the present capacity of Finland and Lapland for the support of the reindeer.

But the routes for reindeer travel must not be laid out in river valleys nor along the coast of the ocean. The reindeer would starve on account of lack of moss. This was the actual experience in the journey made by Mr. Kjellmann in the winter of 1897, from Port Clarence south to Bristol Bay. He accomplished the other parts of his journey, even the scaling of high mountain passes without difficulty, but in attempting to conduct a portion of his return journey through the forest between the Kuskokwim and Yukon rivers he could not find moss enough to subsist his reindeer except by cutting down trees and using an inferior quality of moss. As it was, a half dozen of his deer perished. These reindeer journeys can be accomplished only on trails leading over the hills above the river valleys.

The introduction of reindeer from Siberia into Alaska.—The importation of reindeer from Siberia has settled favorably all the questions of the Alaska problem except the facility of obtaining a supply and the possibility of obtaining it at any time of the year.

The following table shows at a glance the number imported each year already mentioned above:

Year.	Number.	Year.	Number.
1891	16	1895	123
1892	171		
1893	124		
1894	120	Total	554

The 16 reindeer obtained in 1891 were turned loose on Amaknak Island, Unalaska, and have increased, but the exact number is not now known. The other 538 deer have been herded carefully and their present number is 1,466, of which 466 was the increase in fawns in the spring of 1897.

It will be seen by the above table that 538 reindeer purchased during the four years, 1892 to 1895, an average of 134 per annum, have increased to 1,466 deer. It is said that the deer born on the American side are heavier than the average deer imported from Siberia. If the Government herd amounted to 5,000 deer the annual increase would be between 2,000 and 3,000, a sufficient number to stock all the mission stations in Alaska.

The following table shows the location of these deer on June 30, 1897:

	Old deer.	Fawns.	Total.
1. Government herd, Teller Station	343	126	469
2. Cape Nome herd	193	85	278
3. Swedish herd, Golovin Bay	70	40	110
4. Episcopal herd, Golovin Bay	69	40	109
5. Cape Prince of Wales herd	243	124	367
6. Ta-vo-tuk, apprentice, Teller Station	15	11	26
7. Se-keog-look, apprentice, Teller Station	7	5	12
8. Wocksock, apprentice, Teller Station	2	6	
9. Ah-Look, apprentice, Teller Station	3	2	
10. Electoona, apprentice, Teller Station	4	3	
11. Moses, apprentice, Golovin Bay	20	11	31
12. Martin, apprentice, Golovin Bay	12	7	19
13. Okitkon, apprentice, Golovin Bay	10	5	15
14. Tatpan, apprentice, Golovin Bay	7	5	12
Total	1,000	466	1,466

Herds numbered 2 and 5 have been ordered to Point Barrow to relieve suffering whalers. Two hundred deer trained to harness, or as near that number as could be obtained, were ordered on September 22, 1897, to St. Michael by the honorable the Secretary of the Interior to assist in moving supplies to mines in the Yukon Valley.

The following table shows the annual increase and the number received from previous year:

	1891.	1892.	1893.	1894.	1895.	1896.	1897.
Total from previous year			143	323	492	743	1,000
Fawns surviving			79	145	276	357	466
Purchased during summer	16	171	124	120	123		
Total October 1		171	346	588	891	1,100	1,466
Loss			28	23	96	148	100
Carried forward			143	323	492	743	1,000

The herdsmen first imported from Siberia were members of the Indian tribes, superstitious and uncivilized in their habits. Their method of caring for the deer during the time of fawning was not good.

Since obtaining five families (seventeen persons in all) from Lapland in 1894 the training of the reindeer has proceeded more satisfactorily. The Eskimo apprentices, some twenty-five in number, have learned enough to make them good assistant herdsmen and two of them are excellent teamsters; but it would seem that five years' apprenticeship is required to make intelligent people well acquainted with all the methods needed in training the reindeer to harness, in caring for the young, and with the various other arts which are in possession of the herdsmen's families in Finland and Lapland.

The great difficulty, however, in the experiment in northwestern Alaska is the obtaining of efficient herdsmen. Three of the families of Lapps, after remaining the three years agreed upon, have returned to Lapland. While two skilled Lapp herders, with their boys and with Eskimo apprentices, can handle a large herd of 1,000 or 2,000 reindeer, it requires one Laplander to each ten reindeer trained to the harness as teamsters.

The one link necessary for this satisfactory solution of Alaskan problems is the supply of a sufficient number of reindeer trained to the harness and herders and teamsters from Lapland and Finland skilled in the business. While the deer are large and strong the herdsmen and teamsters obtained from Siberia are of little avail. The methods of the Laplanders, which have been tried during the past three years, have proved to be far better than those of the Siberians. They are superior to the Siberians in the management of the reindeer in the harness, in kindness to them, in civilized habits of living (the Laplanders being a Christian people, the Siberians having a low form of fetichism), and in the use of a language that is known to Europeans.

ORPHANAGE AND SCHOOL, WOOD ISLAND, ALASKA.
Woman's American Baptist Home Mission Society.

MILKING REINDEER AT THE MISSION STATION, GOLOVIN BAY, ALASKA.
Swedish Evangelical Mission Covenant of America.
By P. H. Anderson.

Of transportation by dogs, Dr. Jackson says:

The dog in the Arctic seems to be a middle-sized one, with much of the appearance and habits of the wolf. They are a hardy animal, suited to their environment. From five to eight make a good team. They are frequently hitched up tandem. When traveling an attendant usually runs in front, while a second guides the sled. They will make as many miles in a day as the attendant running in front can lead them, and will carry on the sled about 125 pounds to the dog. When traveling they are fed from 1 to 1½ pounds of dry fish per day. When at home they are allowed to forage for themselves. If a sled load of freight is drawn by dogs a second sled load is necessary for carrying provisions for the two teams of dogs, if the journey is a long one. Consequently it is impossible to utilize dogs on journeys very distant from sources of supply of dog food. Since the rapid increase of the white population in Alaska, and the development of the mines, dog transportation has proved entirely inadequate, although the necessity has been so great that the price of dogs has run up to $100 and $200 apiece. A year ago this fall the steamer *Bella* was frozen in at Fort Yukon, 80 miles distant from Circle City. An effort was made to forward the provisions from the steamer by dog teams on the ice to Circle City and Dawson, but the effort failed. It was found impossible to move the food in sufficient quantities and with sufficient speed to supply the miners of the Yukon, and by spring flour had advanced at Dawson City from $50 to $125 per hundred pounds.

The Bureau of Education has been charged with the care of education in Alaska. The object proposed from the beginning by the Commissioners preceding me, General Eaton and Colonel Dawson, has been to provide such education as to prepare the natives to take up the industries and modes of life established in the States by our white population, and by all means not try to continue the tribal life after the manner of the Indians in the western States and Territories. If the natives of Alaska could be taught the English language, be brought under Christian influences by the missionaries and trained into the forms of industry suitable for the Territory, it seems to follow as a necessary result that the white population of Alaska, composed of immigrants from the States, would be able to employ them in their pursuits, using their labor to assist in mining, transportation, and in the production of food. A population of 40,000 natives engaged in reindeer herding and transportation would furnish the contingent needed to complement or make possible the mining industry. After cautious experiments in 1891, 1892, and 1893, and especially after the arrival of the Lapland families as herdsmen in 1894, it has become certain that the experiment will prove a success. A herd of from 100 to 500 reindeer should be placed at each mission station together with a Lapland herdsman who can instruct twenty or thirty apprentices in the management of the deer. The wages for work done in behalf of the mission station, as has been shown, can be paid by the transfer of reindeer to these apprentices, so that after sufficient skill has been acquired the apprentices will have with them the nucleus of a herd of reindeer to commence their career with. They and their sons will by and by take the reindeer trained for harness and find a profitable employment with transportation companies. At home a large herd will accumulate, furnishing food in the form of reindeer milk and reindeer meat.

The following list of missionary stations will show how the entire territory is commanded from these strategical points.

1. On the Arctic are located the following:

	Denomination.	Teachers.
1. Point Barrow	Presbyterian (Government school).	One missionary.
2. Point Hope	Episcopal	Do.
3. Kotzebue Sound	Quaker	Three missionaries.

With herds of from 1,000 to 5,000 at each of these stations as already intimated, there need never be the slightest fear regarding the whalers who are caught in the ice before reaching Bering Strait. If they can not bring their vessels to the protected harbors near by the missionary stations they can at least escape over the ice and obtain sure subsistence until spring time. They can load their vessels, in fact, with supplies from one of these stations and on the breaking up of the ice in the spring continue their whaling voyages.

2. The following missionary stations are located along the coast from Bering Strait to Unalaska in the Bering Sea:

	Denomination.	Teachers.
4. Cape Prince of Wales	Congregational	Two missionaries.
5. St. Lawrence Island	Presbyterian	Do.
6. do	Government school	One teacher.
(Golovin Bay	Swedish Lutheran	Three missionaries.
7. Kangekosook	do	Two missionaries.
8. Unalaklik	do	Do.
9. St. Joseph	Roman Catholic	Seven missionaries.
10. Cape Vancouver	do	Two missionaries.
11. Bethel	Moravian	Five missionaries.
12. Carmel	do	Four missionaries.

It has been shown that stations like those on the Arctic Ocean can all be placed in sufficient communication in the winter months with the States through reindeer expresses sent with the mail to and from Minook, on the middle Yukon, the most distant station being only four days out by the swiftest mail, established by relays, or only sixteen days by the slowest form of reindeer express.

3. The missionary stations on the Yukon are the following:

	Denomination.	Teachers.
13. Igavig	Moravian	Two missionaries.
14. Ibkamute	Roman Catholic	One missionary.
15. Koserefski	do	Eleven missionaries.
16. Sacred Heart	do	
17. Anvik	Episcopal	Three missionaries.
18. Nulato	Roman Catholic	Do.
19. Circle City	Episcopal	Two missionaries.

While the stations on the Arctic Sea are of vital importance for the safety of the whaling fleet, those on the Yukon are of vital importance for transportation in the winter time, and besides the missionary stations there will doubtless spring up many camps of miners from the middle Yukon on to its highest sources and also along all of the tributaries on which gold may be found. It is too much to expect that miners will raise herds of reindeer, or indeed that reindeer can possibly be raised in the immediate vicinity of a mining camp, but the missionary stations removed at a safe distance from these villages can produce hundreds and thousands of reindeer, together with skilled natives who have learned to speak the English language and have acquired the manners and customs of our people. These will become herdsmen and teamsters for the mines.

4. The Aleutian Islands. On one of these (20) Unalaska has a missionary establishment, Methodist, with two missionaries and one Government teacher.

The Aleutian Islands are all said to be moss-bearing, and they should all have herds of reindeer. If not tame, at least a few should be placed on each island to run wild and stock the pastures.

5. The missionary stations along the northern Pacific Coast between Sitka and Unalaska are:

	Denomination.	Teachers.
21. Wood Island	Baptist	Four missionaries.
22. Yakutat	Swedish Lutheran	Three missionaries.
23. Kadiak [1]		One Government teacher.
24. Afognak [1]		Do.
25. Unga [1]		Do.

[1] Government schools.

The voyage from Sitka to Unalaska, almost directly west, is 1,200 miles. Along this coast the above missionary stations are established. Transportation with the interior of Alaska from these stations will be made possible by the possession of reindeer herds.

6. The missionary stations in the Sitka Archipelago at the southeast are:

		Denomination.	Teachers.
26.	{Haines	Presbyterian	Four missionaries.
	{...do	Government school	One teacher.
27.	{Hoonah	Presbyterian	Four missionaries.
	{...do	Government school	One teacher.
28.	Juneau	Presbyterian	Three missionaries.
29.	...do	Episcopal	One missionary.
30.	...do	Roman Catholic	Three missionaries.
31.	{Douglas	Quaker	Do.
	{...do	Two Government schools	Two teachers.
32.	{Sitka	Presbyterian	Twelve missionaries.
	{...do	Two Government schools	Five teachers.
33.	...do	Episcopal	One missionary.
34.	Kake	Quaker	Two missionaries.
35.	{Fort Wrangel	Presbyterian	Do.
	{...do	Government school	One teacher.
36.	{Saxman	Presbyterian	Two teachers.
	{...do	Government school	Do.
37.	{Jackson	Presbyterian	Four missionaries.
	{...do	Government school	One teacher.
38.	Metlakahtla	Independent	One missionary and assistants.

These stations can not at present be used for education in the art of managing the reindeer for the lack of moss fields. It is therefore deemed very important that a large herd of reindeer should be placed as near as possible to this region, namely, at some point northwest of the Lynn Canal, as near as possible to Chilkat. To this place could be sent enterprising and promising young men from the mission schools in the Sitka Archipelago to be trained for teamsters and herdsmen, for it is at this point, as has already been pointed out, that the problem of winter communication with Alaska, so necessary to its Government management, must be solved.

The reindeer transportation must move out from the north of the Lynn Canal at Chilkat or Dyea. There should be an appropriation of $25,000 per annum for the expense of the camp of a reindeer station at this place—that is, as near as possible to the Lynn Canal—although probably the place selected on Alaskan territory for this purpose must be between the headwaters of the Tanana and White rivers, and 300 miles northwest of Chilkat. This herd should be increased from year to year until it amounts to 5,000, in order to hurry forward the work of developing the resources of Alaska by reindeer culture.

The Government may ultimately be able from time to time to dispose of a sufficient number of these reindeer to reimburse the Treasury for the expense incurred. It is desirable, of course, as soon as possible after a demonstration has been made of the practicability of the scheme and its best methods have been discovered, that private enterprise shall take up and carry on the industry, but it is all important that at least one part of the reindeer industry should be kept along its present lines until the natives of Alaska have been elevated from the status of a hunting and fishing civilization to that of farming and grazing. But if the reindeer enterprise gets entirely into the control of private business parties before this is accomplished its benefits may be turned away from the native people. It is therefore very important that the missionary stations shall be supplied with reindeer herds after the plan already inaugurated by this Bureau.

All of which is respectfully submitted.

W. T. HARRIS,
Commissioner.

Hon. CORNELIUS N. BLISS,
Secretary of the Interior.

SCHOOLHOUSE, ST. LAWRENCE ISLAND, 1897. (Page 1603.)

CHAPTER XXXV.

REPORT ON EDUCATION IN ALASKA.

DEPARTMENT OF THE INTERIOR,
BUREAU OF EDUCATION, ALASKA DIVISION,
Washington, D. C., June 30, 1897.

SIR: I have the honor to submit the twelfth annual report of the United States general agent of education in Alaska for the fiscal year ending June 30, 1897.

There is in Alaska a school population of from 8,000 to 10,000; of these, 1,395 were enrolled in the twenty Government schools in operation during the fiscal year.

Circle City.—Miss Anna Fulcomer, teacher; enrollment, 43; population, whites, half-breeds, and natives. The development of the gold mines along the tributaries of the Upper Yukon has within the past two or three years attracted hundreds of miners, some of them with their families, into that region. Feeling the need for school facilities, on January 5, 1896, a mass meeting was held at Circle City, under the Arctic Circle, in the heart of the Birch Creek mining district, and the center of a population of several thousand, at which a petition for a trained public-school teacher was drawn up and subsequently forwarded to the Bureau of Education, and a volunteer lady teacher temporarily engaged. In their letter to the Bureau, the citizens guaranteed that they would erect a schoolhouse before the arrival of a professional teacher in September. To show that they were in earnest, over $1,100 was raised for school purposes and all the ladies in town were by the citizens constituted a school board. It was felt that such zeal should not be checked, and Miss Anna Fulcomer, who had previously done good service in the school at Unalaska, on the Aleutian Islands, was selected as teacher for Circle City.

Miss Fulcomer thus describes her experiences: "I arrived here on August 17, 1896, finding no school building ready for me, and not a vacant house in town in which I could open the school. Consequently, I was obliged to wait, impatiently, until October 1, when the building was under roof; then I opened my school, in spite of the fact that the windows were not in and the doors were not hung. The men worked off and on while I was teaching, but it was not until December 12 that the work stopped. Since that time the schoolhouse has been as snug and comfortable as any place in town. During the winter nearly all the men in town left for the new gold diggings at Klondike, where they were more successful than they had been here. When the ice ran out of the Yukon the third week in May, these men came down the river, packed up their belongings, and moved to Klondike with their families. This is one reason for the sudden decrease in the attendance during May. The other reason is that at last spring sunshine had come.

"For seven months it had been so cold and stormy that the children could have no out-of-doors play life. In May the weather moderated, the sun shone warm and bright, the snow began to melt, ducks, geese, and song birds slowly came, and the children were fairly wild to be out of doors. It seemed almost as much of a sin to keep them in the house as it does to keep our faithful farm animals shut in the dim, musty barn and feed them on dry hay, when they deserve to be out frisking and enjoying the bright sunshine and eating the tender, fresh grass. Many native children dropped out, and I did not blame them. However, I kept on with an attendance of eleven and twelve pupils. But it suddenly grew intensely hot; all kinds of bugs and worms began to wake from their winter's sleep and came crawling out of the moss filling the chinks between the logs—bees, hornets, and our terrible pest, mosquitoes. Sometimes it was enough to make one's flesh creep. With such visitors as these the children could not study, so before long we had to stop school.

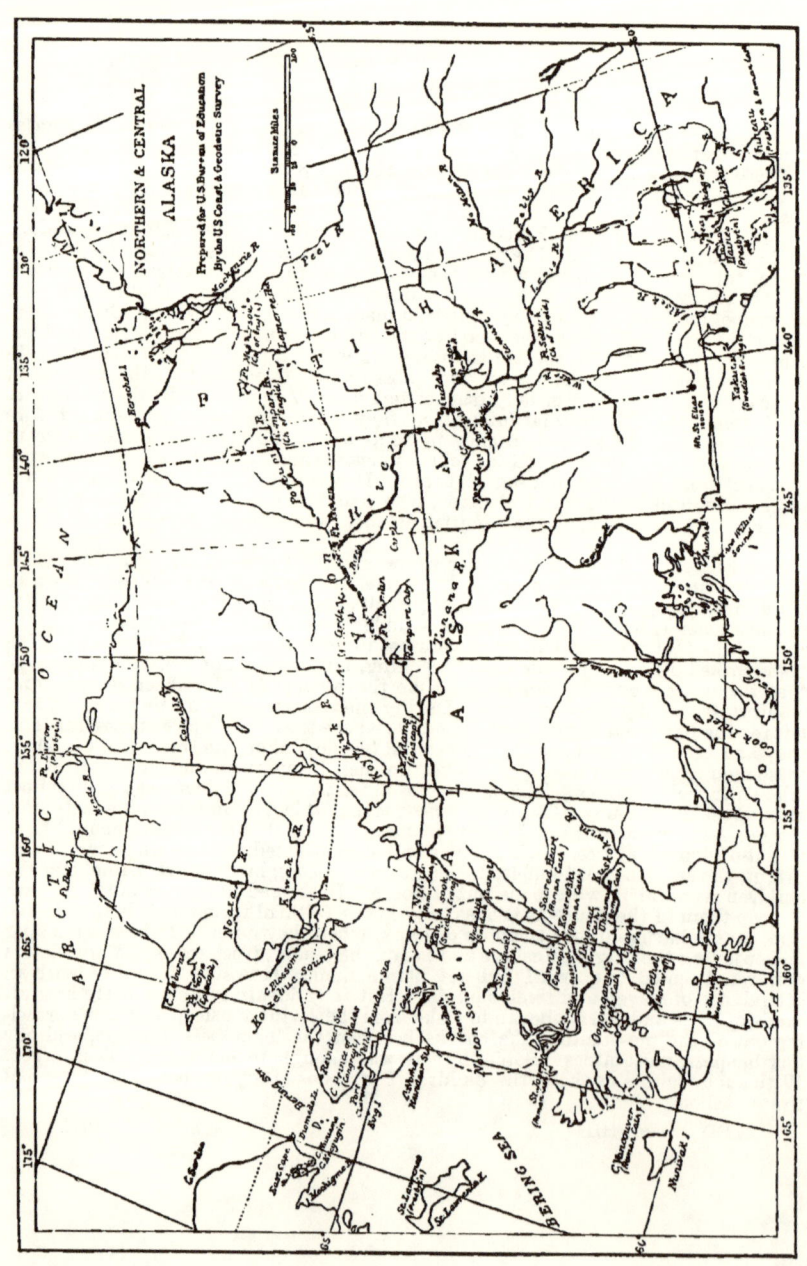

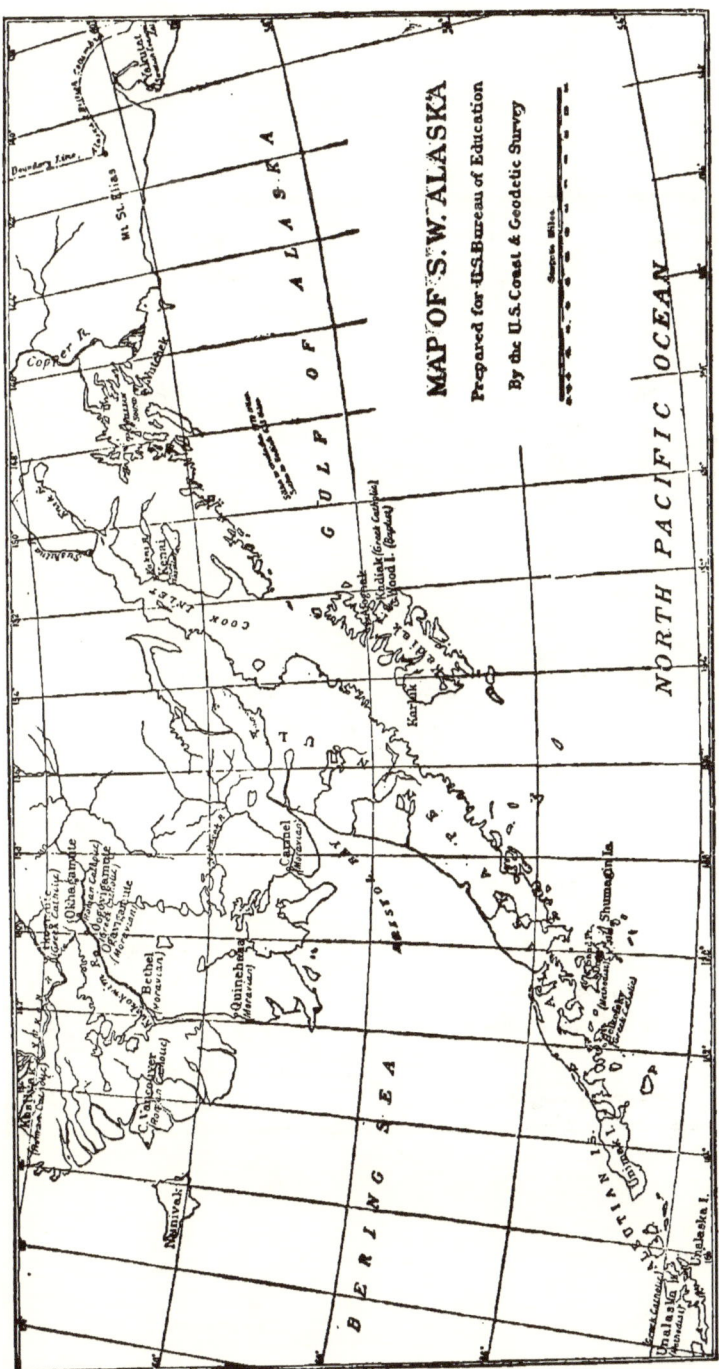

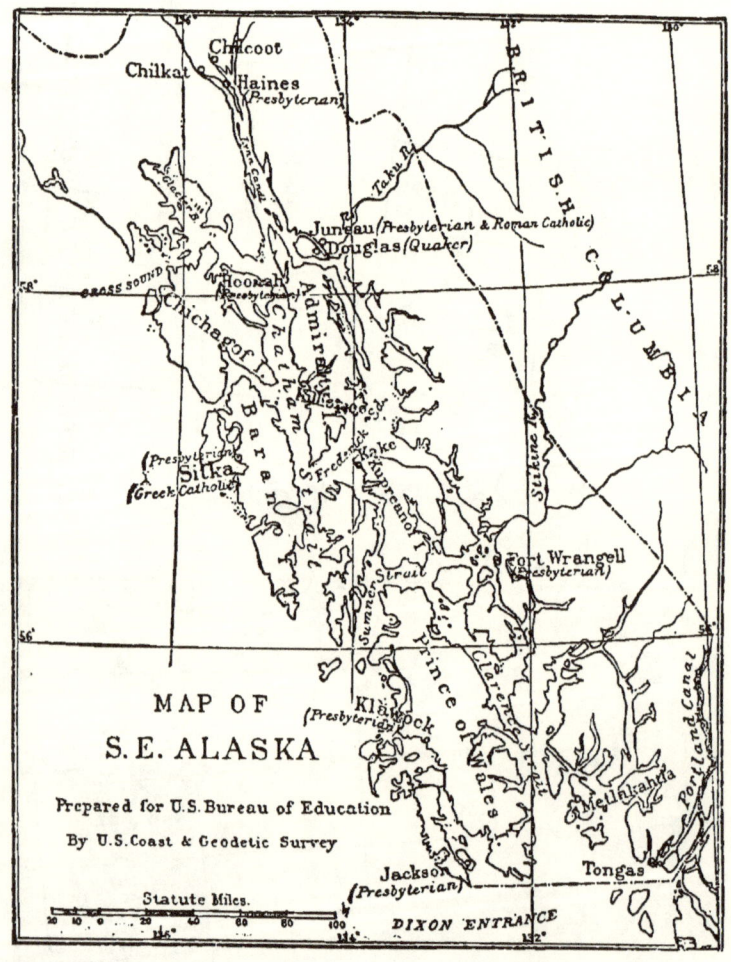

"Teaching school in this far north land is altogether different from teaching in the States, and the teacher is at times compelled to change the usual order of things and use her own judgment, depending on the Department's having faith enough in her to sanction such changes. For nearly three months during the winter the people want to hibernate. They can not help it, for there seems to be something in the air tending to that result. The days are so short that the people sink into a kind of stupor, not wanting to rouse up when daylight comes, even though that be delayed until 11 in the morning. During these dark months I was always at the schoolhouse before half past 9, but was usually alone there until half past 10, when the children would straggle sleepily in, some without breakfast. By noon all would be there.

"When the citizens wrote to the Bureau of Education a year ago for a teacher there was the greatest enthusiasm on the subject; but months before I arrived all the enthusiasm had died out, the women trustees were at sword's points, nearly all the money raised had been paid out for the temporary teacher and firewood, and hardly anyone, even those who had children, were in favor of a school at all, but wanted the money that remained put into a hall for town and dance purposes. However, the school has been a success. I like the children; the majority are bright, intelligent, and lovable."

Teller Reindeer Station.—T. L. Brevig, teacher; enrollment of pupils, 53; population, Eskimo. During the fiscal year school has been in session one hundred and sixty days. The attendance has been somewhat less than during the previous year, owing to the fact that the headquarters of the herd has been at Ageeopak, which was too far from the station to permit the regular attendance of the herders. The progress made among those who attended regularly has been satisfactory. It has been noticed that the Eskimos who have been to the States one or more times are far ahead of the rest of the natives with regard to cleanliness, clothing, language, and good behavior. This is the natural result of contact with civilization.

Cape Prince of Wales.—Thomas Hanna, teacher; enrollment of pupils, 132; population, Eskimo. The school was not so well attended as in previous years. A feud between two of the principal families, brought about by drunkenness and the killing of two men and the scarcity of food were the chief causes of the decreased attendance. School work was so divided that both day and night sessions were held. The printing press donated by Mrs. W. T. Hatch, of Brooklyn, N. Y., has been very useful in enabling the teacher to prepare supplementary lessons for the school. Some of the boys have assisted in setting type and in distributing it. A kindergarten was established in May, conducted by Mrs. Lopp.

St. Lawrence Island.—V. C. Gambell, teacher; enrollment of pupils, 66; population, Eskimo. The people, young and old, have shown untiring interest in the school. On stormy days the parents carry the smaller children to school. We let all the children come, no difference how young they are, but they are not enrolled if under 5; these learn English and songs from hearing the older ones. The girls attend regularly now, though they are yet very bashful. The winds were unusually favorable the past winter, allowing them to catch an abundance of seals: so that at no time was there suffering from lack of food.

They have at last learned to manufacture whisky. A whaler brought a woman from Point Hope who taught them. They use about 5 quarts of molasses and 3 of flour to a 5-gallon coal oil can of water. This is allowed to ferment for from four to seven days, when it is heated, the vapor passing through an old gun barrel which is kept cool, thus condensing it. This yields about a quart of whisky. Several houses were making it all winter, and drunken men were not uncommon.

The children are cleaner, and show a decided improvement in every way. We try to have all the people clean themselves up when the *Bear* comes, and a great many of them do in their way. We think we have gained their confidence, and look forward for greater improvements in the not distant future.

Unalaska.—Miss M. E. Mellor, teacher, and Miss M. Salamatoff, assistant; enrollment, 48; population, Aleut. Miss Mellor reports as follows: "The school opened September 1, 1896, with an enrollment of 39 children; 48 were on the roll at the close of school. This represents the number of regular attendants only. At intervals during the year we had an attendance of 56 for a week at a time—almost all the children in the village. When the Russian school closed for the holidays many of the boys came to our school regularly during that time. They seemed to prefer the 'American' school, as they called it, and when they came to ask permission to attend, if only for a short season, we had not the heart to refuse them, although we were overcrowded without them. For over a month we had two children from the distant island of Sannakh. Their mother brought them to me, and, through an interpreter, asked if I would take them into our school. The children, as a whole, have worked well at their studies, and their progress has been encouraging. In arithmetic the highest class has commenced work in fractions, and almost half of the pupils can do examples in multiplication and long division with a very fair degree of accuracy and rapidity. Much attention has been given to phonic drill and to the construction of English sentences. We have exercises in composition three times a week, some familiar object being taken; and after reading or talking about it the children would write on their slates what they could remember about it. These written exercises were read aloud in class and criticised, both as to subject-matter and the use of English. We have no text-books on United States history, but I read to the older pupils from a 'Young Folks' history and then talked about it. Marked progress has been made in reading; each class has had two lessons a day. It is gratifying to note an increasing love for the study. Elementary drawing, physiology, and geography have also had their proper place in school work, with gratifying results. The work of the year has been very pleasant and the outlook is most encouraging."

Unga.—O. R. McKinney, teacher; enrollment, 40; population, white and Aleut. Mr. McKinney submits the following report: "During the summer, authority was granted by the Commissioner of Education for the building of an extension to the schoolhouse, to be used as a library room. Owing to the fact that we could not secure the services of a carpenter, I commenced school on August 24, in order to get in as much time as possible before the carpenter was ready. I continued school until the last of September. I then closed school and set to work with the carpenter at the building, so that it might be finished as soon as possible. About the last of October we had the work far enough along to enable us to have school again. During the holidays the carpenter completed the work, and from January 10 our school continued until May 30 without interruption. My pupils are making rapid progress in their studies, and we seem to have the full sympathy and support of all the patrons. On March 12 we had an exhibition, which was considered a grand success. The school is in better condition than ever before, the moral tone of our village has been much better during the year than ever, and there is nothing to discourage me in my work. Our library is still increasing, and is doing a great deal of good among the readers. Books will be thankfully received. We are much in need of an organ or some musical instrument in our school."

Kadiak.—C. C. Solter, teacher; enrollment, 52; population, Russian Creoles. Mr. Solter writes: "My larger pupils did excellent work in language and drawing. I am sometimes surprised to get such well-written sentences, when I consider that outside of the schoolroom scarcely a word of English is spoken. In drawing they excel, and make better progress than the average American children. In arithmetic they are not so apt, yet I have third-reader pupils who handle fractions very readily. They take much interest also in geography and history. If anyone doubts whether it pays for these children to attend school, the parents of the children certainly do not. They want their children to learn, and are proud to receive a letter from an absent son or daughter.

"Many children who live in settlements where there is no school would be sent here if we could board them. I have been asked several times by white men to take in their boy or girl, that he or she could have the benefit of an education. So far it has been impossible for us to accommodate anyone, though the parents were willing to pay board for their children. There is no place here where a child could be properly cared for; all the people have enough to do to take care of their own children. Our house is too small. If we did take them we would soon be overcrowded in our schoolroom, which is barely large enough to accommodate the Kadiak children. There is no doubt that if a boarding school were started the children would flock in from all parts of this district. This would be the most satisfactory kind of a school. There would be regularity in attendance. Being in school constantly, they would soon learn to use the English language fluently, to the exclusion of the Russian and Aleut. They would thus exercise an influence for good over the other children and become thoroughly Americanized. Several families now live in Kadiak in order that their children may have the advantage of the school. The fathers are at work at distant stations. Many more would do the same thing if they could afford it. Every year I furnish a number of books to parents living at a distance, who begin the education of their children at home. I hope that Congress will increase our appropriations until in the near future every child in Alaska may have a chance for a common-school education. I can not close my report without urging again the necessity of compulsory attendance. The Russian schools are able to compel attendance by the authority of the church, but American teachers can only urge the advantages to be secured with indifferent success. Some resident of the village should be appointed with full authority to enforce the attendance of all recalcitrant young-

MATRON AND PUPILS, JESSE LEE HOME, UNALASKA.
Woman's Home Mission Society of the Methodist Episcopal Church.

TEACHER AND PUPILS, INDUSTRIAL GROUP, SITKA.
Woman's Board of Home Missions of the Presbyterian Church.

sters. The children were very much pleased with the garden seeds that were kindly sent me by the Bureau for distribution among their parents. At first I gave a package of seeds to one child in each family, thinking that would be sufficient, but the rest thought themselves slighted and wept so piteously that I had to give each child a package. They evidently made good use of them, as small gardens can be seen scattered all over town. Many of them had never planted seeds before."

Karluk.—R. B. Dunmire, teacher; enrollment, 28; population, whites and Aleuts. The school year has shown decided progress in the various branches of school work. The people are learning to discriminate between Americans and the fishermen and sailors who come to this great canning station during the summer months. Of course, the opposition of the Russian Church is as decided as ever. The children have been better clad than they were last winter, still some of them come to school in their bare feet even on cold days. The population is decreasing rapidly, owing largely to the poverty of the natives, coupled with their drunkenness and immorality. The fishermen are the chief cause of these two vices. Of the children born during the last two years, but one remains alive. The United States commissioner at Unalaska, 700 miles away, is the nearest representative of the authority of the United States. Here there is no means whatever of punishing the perpetrators of crime. Still there is hope for the children in that they are rapidly learning the English language and are beginning to learn how to take care of themselves. It is yet possible to repair some of the wrong that has been done them.

Haines.—W. W. Warne, teacher; enrollment, 68; population. Thlinget. Mr. Warne writes: "This report closes the sixth year of my services as teacher of this school. The year has been our best. More real advancement has been made than in any previous year; the attendance has not been much larger, but it has been more regular and we have not had so many raw recruits. Most of the children around here have been to school more or less, so that instead of it being the exception to find a child that has attended school it is now the exception to find one who has not attended, at least for a short time. If we continue work a few years longer, we shall have reached almost all the children, and our work will be firmly established. In my experience with the parents I can not help but notice that they begin to regard it as a disgrace for a child to remain illiterate, and all show more or less eagerness to have their children attend school. The change in this respect during the past six years is very noticeable. I see a bright future for our work, although I can not deny that there is a dark side, but the progress certainly has been encouraging, and I hope that the good work may be pushed even more rapidly in the future than it has been in the past."

Sitka, No 1.—Mrs. G. Knapp, teacher; enrollment, 39; population, white, American, and Russian. The regularity of attendance at this school has been very satisfactory, largely owing to the fact that the teacher offered prizes for punctuality. Because of the many changes among the naval and civil officials stationed at Sitka there are changes in the school. Children from the States come and go with their parents, and it is possible to compare the work of the school with the work done in cities in the East. Mrs. Knapp states that children from the States enter classes with Sitka children of their own age. A circulating library is maintained in connection with the school, and has proved a source of much enjoyment to the children.

Sitka, No. 2.—Miss Cassia Patton, teacher, and Miss Flora Campbell, assistant; enrollment, 154; population, Thlinget. The following is Miss Patton's report: "There being two teachers, we were able to give more individual instruction, which is especially helpful to these non-English speaking children. Our girls and small boys enjoyed knitting very much. In sewing, we found some of the girls quite apt in the use of the needle, and the boys were pleased to learn how to sew on buttons, especially when they were allowed to replace any lost from their garments. Much of our work is developing their knowledge of English, which is not spoken in their homes. I have a small collection of objects by which they are surrounded at home, of which they soon learn the English names. About the 1st of November the Russian parochial school opened and took from us some of the children who were faithful followers of the Russo-Greek Church, but many continued to go to both schools irregularly in order to be sure of two Christmas trees. One day the janitor of the Russian school came into our school and asked for all the 'Russian Indians,' as followers of the Greek Church are called. I replied (Miss Campbell interpreting) that I did not distinguish between Russian Indians or any other kind, and that this was a Government public school, where all were on the same footing. He began picking them out; then I told him that they were all Americans and could come here if they pleased. Taking the flag, which we are in the habit of saluting. I spoke to the children and told them that if their parents wished them to come to this school no one else had anything to say about it. I was only sorry that I could not say to the parents that according to the laws of the United States they must send their children to learn English, or American, as they term it. In January there was great feasting and dancing in the native village in honor of the visit of a hundred visitors from Hoonah, which interfered considerably with our attendance. Then came an epidemic of whooping cough and the usual spring exodus for fish eggs. Immediately after Christmas I offered prizes to be given on Washington's Birthday to those whose attendance was good until that time; seven were worthy of dolls or mouth organs, and one, whose record was excellent, I deemed worthy of a suit of clothes, and a very happy boy he was, for I believe it was his first whole new suit. My next effort to increase the attendance and punctuality was to buy a number of toys which I allowed the children to play with before each session.

"For the last three years I have distributed garden seeds during the last months of school, thus keeping the children in attendance and interesting the parents. Through the kindness of Dr. Jackson and the Agricultural Department, I was able to distribute a greater quantity this year. In this work I have been very much assisted by my father, who is a practical farmer, and has allowed me to bring my classes to his garden, where he showed them how to plant and weed. The great drawback to their gardening is that they have had the habit of planting on distant islands, only visiting them from time to time. A beginning has now been made in making gardens in the Sitka village. If they continue to do this, I believe it will tend to make them build their houses farther apart, which will be an improvement from a sanitary point of view and perhaps tend to break up the custom of several families living in the same house. I have yet a further interest in this gardening. My father is experimenting in the raising of flax, which, I believe, is just the thing for this country. I have had a wooden loom built, which the natives, who are apt with tools, can copy, and I propose to teach the women to weave rag carpet. These carpets will make their homes more attractive; and if the flax is a success, the industries of gardening and weaving will be open to them. Of course this will be slow work, but as the fishing and hunting diminish we need to have industries in which they are interested ready for them."

Juneau, No. 1.—S. A. Keller, teacher: enrollment, 86; population, white. Juneau is the largest town in southeast Alaska, and the school is working on a course that will soon reach the high-school grade. However, with only one teacher it is difficult to plan the work so as to give each pupil the training necessary for individual intellectual growth. About 20 per cent of the children of school age are on the streets. A law for compulsory regular attendance at school would be a great benefit.

Juneau, No. 2.—Miss Elizabeth Saxman, teacher; enrollment, 26; population, Thlinget. Miss Saxman writes: "The spirit of emulation that prevailed among the children during the entire term was indeed encouraging. The boys and girls seemed more wide-awake and enthusiastic than ever before. More than a little rivalry was manifested. The lack of this used to annoy me considerably, as some of the largest pupils did not seem to care whether they made any progress or not. In many cases it is difficult to get the native parents to send their children to school. They give you faithful promises when you go to see them, and say that they will send their children 'to-morrow' or 'next week'—in fact, say anything to settle the question for the present. However, I feel that we shall surely reach them satisfactorily this winter, since Mr. Fred Moore (a native graduate of the Sitka school) has been appointed chief of the native police. He is doing a grand work among his people."

Jackson.—Miss C. Baker, teacher; enrollment, 84; population, Thlinget. Miss Baker reports as follows: "At the commencement of the term but few of the natives had returned from their summer hunting. After the village had filled up I went around and talked with each family of the importance of sending the children to school regularly. As a result, every child in town that was large enough came to school. I used every effort to increase their interest and keep them in school, and succeeded beyond my expectations, the irregularity in the cases in which it occurred being the fault of the parents and not of the children. We have kept the schoolroom well filled, well cleaned, and well ventilated throughout the term. The interest and progress have been commendable, arithmetic and writing being the favorite studies. The discouraging feature of the work is the continual coming and going of the natives from village to village, which greatly interferes with regularity of attendance. However, I think we have had an excellent school."

Fort Wrangel.—Miss Anna R. Kelsey, teacher; enrollment, 64; population,

Thlinget. This is the oldest of the schools in Alaska, having been established in 1877. From that time until the present it has continued to be a means for the uplifting of the natives in this region. Here the native chief, Shakes, has been of considerable assistance in securing the attendance of the children.

Saxman.—J. W. Young, teacher; Miss M. J. Young, assistant teacher: enrollment, 75; population, Thlinget. Mr. Young gives the following account of the year: "The year has made a great change in the size of the community, and if that is to be a test, we have succeeded very well. When I arrived here in the fall of 1895 to build up a temperance, self-governing community there was no building here except the schoolhouse. Now we have a village of 24 houses, with a population of 120. As you know, the Thlingets do not remain in one place during the entire year, but go to their hunting and fishing grounds at the proper season. During the months of December, January, and February we had quite a good school, and the pupils made good progress in their studies, especially the younger ones. Some of them did not know a single letter when they came in the fall and now they are in the Second Reader. We find it difficult to get the older ones to attend with any degree of regularity, consequently their progress is slow.

"We have had some encouragements in our work. The natives have been very kind and even generous to us, doing what they could to make it pleasant for us. But we have had some discouragements as well. Although we have succeeded in keeping intoxicating liquor out of the village, yet the effects of its use elsewhere have reached us. In February the natives became intoxicated at Ketchikan, and in a drunken fight a Cape Fox native struck a Tongas native on the head with a rifle, from the effects of which he died. The Tongas tribe demanded pay for the life of their tribesman and the Cape Fox people gave them 200 blankets. Then the Tongas men demanded the life of a Cape Fox chief, as the murdered man had been a chief. The Cape Fox tribe refused, and their warriors armed themselves to resist the threatened attack of the Tongas men. Some of the latter came down from Ketchikan in their war paint, with rifles and knives, bent on killing. The women and children crowded into the schoolhouse, in terror. However, when the attacking party found that our people were ready for them and determined to make a stout resistance, they returned without firing a shot. This trouble is very unfortunate for Saxman, as it has made hard feeling between the two tribes that we were gathering together, and I fear will keep a number of the Tongas people from coming to Saxman.

"I found that there was great need for a store in our new settlement, so I put up a suitable building and sent for my son, who laid in a stock of goods and is conducting a successful business. It is a great help to the community."

TABLE I.—*General statement of the expenditure of all appropriations*

	1884.	1884–85.	1885–86.	1886–87.	1887–88.	1888–89.
Original fund to establish schools in Alaska	$25,000.00					
Balance original fund, forward		$25,000.00	$24,562.23	$11,083.23	$3,443.83	
Annual appropriation				15,000.00	25,000.00	$40,000.00
From fund for education of Indians						
Special appropriation for Circle City school						
Total amount available each year		25,000.00	24,562.23	26,083.23	28,443.83	40,000.00
Salaries of teachers			4,868.43	11,935.97	11,940.00	10,482.72
Salaries of officials			267.05	1,200.00	1,200.00	1,450.00	1,920.74
School supplies and equipment			155.87	4,262.53	3,313.80	2,636.66	1,596.59
Freight charges			14.85	492.29	4,710.45	214.60	18.00
Repairs, care of buildings, etc				125.75	377.14	160.50	
Rents				280.00	310.00		220.00
Incidentals					71.72	110.71	130.35
Traveling expenses					189.32	574.90	220.00
Construction of buildings					231.00	5,873.45	7,410.00
Contract schools				2,250.00	300.00	1,300.00	18,000.00
Total expenditure		437.77	13,479.00	22,639.40	24,260.82	39,998.40
Balance original fund carried over	25,000.00	24,562.23	11,083.23	3,443.83		
Balance all other appropriations unexpended					4,183.01	1.60
Cost of public schools, not including cost of buildings and contract schools		437.77	11,229.00	22,108.40	17,067.37	14,588.40
Cost per capita of enrollment			23.06	19.33	19.09	15.91

made by the Government for education in Alaska from 1884 to 1897.

1889–90.	1890–91.	1891–92.	1892–93.	1893–94.	1894–95.	1895–96.	1896–97.	Total.
								$25,000.00
$50,000.00	$50,000.00	$50,000.00	$40,000.00	$30,000.00	$30,000.00	$30,000.00	$30,000.00	390,000.00
					5,000.00	5,000.00	5,000.00	15,000.00
							1,500.00	1,500.00
50,000.00	50,000.00	50,000.00	40,000.00	30,000.00	35,000.00	35,000.00	36,500.00	431,500.00
9,797.43	12,891.07	12,215.07	13,758.00	14,395.60	17,909.39	22,062.42	21,293.72	163,749.82
2,139.00	2,954.19	3,280.00	3,280.00	2,880.00	3,028.30	3,180.00	3,580.00	30,159.37
2,670.81	2,944.13	3,098.22	2,244.56	2,136.02	2,939.03	3,359.13	5,544.24	36,901.59
72.00	319.54		338.28		1,371.34	32.55	64.04	7,647.94
	30.00	427.30	768.00	1,411.37	1,585.55	223.14	574.61	5,683.36
90.00	200.00			200.00	200.00	200.00	225.00	1,925.00
448.50			11.00	14.00	32.07	325.26	183.18	1,326.79
444.60	573.55	1,003.76	1,511.55	783.56	1,527.47	1,097.20	683.88	8,609.79
1,500.00	1,726.86		1,000.00		3,435.25	3,510.00	1,850.00	26,536.56
31,174.12	28,360.61	28,980.00	17,040.00	8,000.00				135,404.73
48,336.55	49,999.95	49,004.35	39,951.39	29,820.55	32,028.40	33,989.70	33,998.67	417,944.95
1,663.45	.05	995.65	48.61	179.45	a2,971.60	a1,010.30	a2,501.33	13,555.05
15,662.43	19,912.48	20,024.35	21,012.39	21,820.55	28,593.15	30,479.70	32,148.67	256,003.66
20.50	26.73	25.09	27.60	27.04	27.76	25.46	25.00	23.02

a These balances are reserved awaiting the acceptance of the school building at Unalaska.

TABLE II.—*Statistics of public*

Public schools.	1885-86.		1886-87.		1887-88.		1888-89.		1889-90.	
	Months taught.	Enrollment.	Months taught.	Enrollment.	Months taught.	Enrollment.	Months taught.	Enrollment.	Months taught.	Enrollment.
Afognak			9	35	9	24	9	55	8	33
Douglas City No. 1		(a)		(a)	9	67	9	94	5	50
Douglas City No. 2		(a)		(a)		(a)		(a)	8	62
Fort Wrangel	9	50	9	106	9	106	9	90	9	83
Haines	9	84	6	43	8	114	8	128		(a)
Jackson	9	87	9	123	9	110	9	105	9	87
Juneau No. 1	9	96	9	236	9	25	9	36	9	31
Juneau No. 2		(a)		(a)	9	67	9	58	9	51
Kadiak			9	59	9	81	9	68	9	67
Karluk		(a)		(a)		(a)		(a)		(a)
Killisnoo	5	50	9	125	9	44	9	40	9	32
Klawock			6	184	9	81	9	75	2	68
Kake										
Sitka No. 1	9	43	9	60	9	60	9	67	9	58
Sitka No. 2	6	77	9	138	9	60	9	51	9	83
Unga		(a)	9	35	9	26		(a)	9	24
Unalaska										
Port Clarence		(a)		(a)		(a)		(a)		(a)
Metlakahtla										
St. Lawrence Island										
Saxman										
Hoonah										
Cape Prince of Wales										
Circle City										
Point Barrow										
Total		487		1,144		895		917		764

a No school.

NOTE.—In addition to supporting the above public schools, the Bureau of Education pays the salaries of three industrial teachers in the Sitka Industrial School, which has an enrollment of 150.

EDUCATION IN ALASKA.

schools in Alaska from 1885 to 1897.

Length of school term and enrollment of pupils each year.														
1890-91.		1891-92.		1892-93.		1893-94.		1894-95.		1895-96.		1896-97.	
Months taught.	Enrollment.	Months taught.	Enrollment.	Months taught.	Enrollment.	Months taught.	Enrollment.	Months taught.	Enrollment.	Months taught.	Enrollment.	Months taught.	Enrollment.
9	37	7	35	8	40	9	38	9	38	9	29		(a)
9	23	9	25	8	13	9	30	9	42	9	57	7	75
9	68	9	24	9	109	9	87	7	26		(a)	8	32
9	93	9	49	9	49	9	54	8	61	9	82	9	64
	(a)	9	89	9	54	9	41	9	64	8	60	9	68
9	100	9	100	9	82	8	90	7	80	8	64	9	81
9	33	9	26	9	23	9	25	9	54	9	70	9	86
9	51	9	75	9	61	9	65	9	50	9	67	9	70
9	80	9	69	9	74	9	59	9	56	8	49	9	52
9	33	9	29		(a)		(a)		(a)	9	27	9	23
9	68	2	33	9	137	5	75		(a)		(a)		(a)
7	50	2	38		(a)		(a)	2	50		(a)		(a)
		3	60										
9	54	9	50	9	50	7	43	9	57	9	40	9	39
8	55	9	54	9	48	9	110	9	180	9	156	9	154
	(a)	8	33	8	35	9	36	9	40	9	44	9	40
						9	24	9	39	9	39	9	48
	(a)		(a)	5	20	7	30	8	56	9	56	9	53
								6	105		(a)		(a)
								7	52	9	68	9	66
										7	31	8	75
										8	144	5	120
										9	104	7	132
											(a)	8	43
												6	66
	745		798		794		807		1,030		1,197		1,395

TABLE III.—*Erection of school buildings in Alaska.*

Public schools.	Cost.	Character.	Dimensions.	Date of payment.	Fund from which paid.
			Feet.		
Sitka, No. 1 (whites).	$2,000.00	Frame, 1 story.	33½ x 40	May 5, 1888	1884. Original fund to establish schools in Alaska.
Killisnoo (natives)	231.00	...do. a		June 29, 1887	Do.
Sitka, No. 2 (natives).	1,537.20	...do	39¼ x 25¼	Dec. 14, 1888	1887-88. Fund, education of children in Alaska.
Juneau, No. 1 (whites)	2,336.25	...do	33½ x 40	Oct. 23, 1888	Do.
Juneau, No. 2 (natives).	1,300.00	...do	30 x 60	Oct. 13, 1894	1894-95. Fund, education of children in Alaska.
Douglas, No.1(whites)	1,200.00	...do	30 x 20	May 7, 1890	1888-89. Fund, education of children in Alaska.
Douglas (Treadwell mine) (whites).	1,730.00	...do	30 x 60	Oct. 24, 1896	1895-96. Fund, education of Indians.
Kake (natives)	376.86	Log, 1 story	20 x 30	July 18, 1891	1890-91. Fund, education of children in Alaska.
Saxman (natives)	1,780.00	Frame, 1 story.	30 x 60	Nov. 27, 1895	1895-96. Fund, education of Indians.
Chilkat (natives)	350.00	Log, 1 story	20 x 30	July 22, 1891	1890-91. Fund, education of children in Alaska.
Hoonah (natives)	1,850.00	Frame, 1 story.	30 x 60	Sept. 8, 1897	1895-97. Fund, education of Indians.
Kadiak (whites and natives).	2,700.00	...do	20 x 30	Dec. 6, 1890	1888-89 and 1889-90. Funds, education of children in Alaska.
Afognak (whites and natives).	2,505.00	...do	20 x 46	...do	1888-89. Fund, education of children in Alaska.
Karluk (whites and natives).	2,505.00	...do	20 x 46	...do	Do.
Unalaska (natives)	2,135.25	Frame, 1½ stories.	55 x 31	Oct. 28, 1895	1894-95. Fund, education of Indians.
St. Lawrence Island (natives).	1,000.00	Frame, 1 story.	20 x 40	Oct. 31, 1891	1890-91. Fund. Leducation of children in Alaska.
Port Clarence (natives).	1,000.00	Log, 1 story	22 x 32	Jan. 31, 1893	1892-93. Fund, education of children in Alaska.
Total cost	26,536.56				

a Burned February 18, 1894.

Appropriations for education in Alaska.

First grant to establish schools, 1884 .... $25,000
Annual grants, school year—
  1886-87 15,000
  1887-88 25,000
  1888-89 40,000
  1889-90 50,000
  1890-91 50,000
  1891-92 50,000
  1892-93 40,000
  1893-94 30,000
  1894-95 30,000
  1895-96 30,000
  1896-97 30,000

PERSONNEL.

Dr. Sheldon Jackson, Alaska, general agent of education in Alaska; William Hamilton, Pennsylvania, assistant agent of education in Alaska; William A. Kelly, Pennsylvania, superintendent of schools for the southeastern district of Alaska.

LOCAL SCHOOL COMMITTEES.

Sitka, Edward de Groff, Charles D. Rogers, John G. Brady; Juneau, John G. Heid, Karl Koehler; Douglas, P. H. Fox, Albert Anderson; Treadwell, Robert Duncan, jr., Rev. A. J. Campbell; Fort Wrangel, Thomas Wilson, Finis Cagle; Kadiak, Nicolai Kashevaroff, F. Sargent, H. P. Cope; Unga, C. M. Dederick, Michael Dowd, George Levitt.

EDUCATION IN ALASKA.

Teachers in public schools.

School.	Teacher.	State.
Sitka, No. 1	Mrs. Gertrude Knapp	Pennsylvania.
Sitka, No. 2	Miss Cassia Patton	Do.
	Miss Flora Campbell	Alaska.
Juneau, No. 1	S. A. Keller	Indiana.
Juneau, No. 2	Miss Elizabeth Saxman	Pennsylvania.
Hoonah	Mrs. A. R. McFarland	Alaska.
Douglas, No. 1	Miss Anna Hunnicutt	California.
Douglas, No. 2	Miss K. T. Williams	Do.
Fort Wrangel	Miss Anna R. Kelsey	Pennsylvania.
Jackson	Miss C. Baker	Alaska.
Saxman	J. W. Young	Washington.
	Miss M. J. Young	Do.
Haines	Rev. W. W. Warne	New Jersey.
Kadiak	C. C. Solter	Kansas.
Karluk	R. B. Dunmire	New Jersey.
Unga	O. R. McKinney	Pennsylvania.
Unalaska	Miss M. E. Mellor	New York.
	Miss M. Salamatoff	Alaska.
Port Clarence	T. L. Brevig	Minnesota.
St. Lawrence Island	V. C. Gambell	Iowa.
Cape Prince of Wales	Thomas Hanna	California.
Circle City	Miss Anna Fulcomer	Nebraska.
Point Barrow	L. M. Stevenson	Ohio.
Sitka Industrial School	F. E. Frobese	Germany.
	Geo. J. Beck	New York.
	Miss Olga Hilton	Alaska.

TEACHERS AND EMPLOYEES IN CHURCH MISSION SCHOOLS.

Episcopalians.

Point Hope.—J. B. Driggs, M. D., Rev. H. E. Edson.
Anvik.—Rev. and Mrs. J. W. Chapman, Miss Bertha W. Sabine.
Fort Adams.—Rev. and Mrs. Jules L. Prevost, Mary V. Glenton, M. D.
Juneau.—Rev. Henry Beer.
Douglas Island.—Rev. A. J. Campbell.
Sitka.—Bishop Peter Trimble Rowe.
Circle City.—Rev. R. Bowen.

Congregational.

Cape Prince of Wales.—Mr. and Mrs. W. T. Lopp, Rev. and Mrs. Thomas Hanna.

Roman Catholic.

Kosyrevsky.—Rev. R. Crimont, S. J., and Brothers Rosati, S. J.; Marchesio, S. J.; Cunningham, S. J.; Sisters M. Stephen, M. Joseph, M. Winfred, M. Anguilbert, M. Heloise, and M. Damascene.
Nulato.—Rev. A. Ragaru, S. J.; Rev. F. Monroe, S. J., and Brother Giordano, S. J.
Shageluk.—Rev. William Judge, S. J.
Urhhamute, Kuskokwim River.—Rev. A. Robant, S. J.
St. Josephs, Yukon Delta.—Rev. J. Treca, S. J.; Rev. A. Parodi, S. J.; Rev. F. Barnum, S. J.; Brothers Twohigg, S. J., and Negro, S. J., and Sisters M. Zypherine, M. Benedict, M. Prudence, and M. Pauline.
Juneau.—Rev. J. B. Rene and Sisters Mary Zeno, M. Peter, and M. Bousecour.

Moravians.

Bethel.—Rev. and Mrs. John H. Kilbuck, Mr. and Mrs. Benjamin Helmick, Miss Mary Mack, Mr. and Mrs. J. H. Romig, M. D.
Quiegaluk.—Mr. Ivan Harrison (Eskimo).
Tulaksagamute.—Mr. and Mrs. David Skuvink (Eskimos).
Kalchkachagamute.—Mr. and Mrs. George Nukachluk (Eskimos).

Akaigamiut.—Mr. Neck (Eskimo).
Ugavig.—Rev. and Mrs. Ernst L. Webber.
Quinchaha.—Mr. L. Kawagleg and Mr. and Mrs. Harvey Suruka (Eskimos).
Carmel.—Rev. and Mrs. John Schoechert, Rev. S. H. Rock, Misses Mary and Emma Huber, Miss P. C. King.

Methodist Episcopal.

Unalaska.—Miss Agnes S. Sowle, Miss Sarah J. Rinch, Miss Ada Mellor.

Friends.

Douglas City.—Mr. and Mrs. C. N. Reploge. (No report.)
Kake.—Mr. and Mrs. S. R. Moon. (No report.)

Baptists.

Wood Island.—Rev. and Mrs. Curtis P. Coe, Miss Alice Thompson.

Presbyterian.

Point Barrow.—L. M. Stevenson.
St. Lawrence Island.—Mr. and Mrs. V. C. Gambell.
Haines.—Rev. and Mrs. W. W. Warne, Miss Anna M. Sheets, Miss Fannie H. Willard (native).
Hoonah.—Rev. and Mrs. Alvin C. Austin, Mrs. John W. McFarland, and Mrs. Mary E. Howell.
Juneau.—Rev. and Mrs. James H. Condit, Rev. and Mrs. L. F. Jones, Miss Sue Davis, Miss M. E. Gould, Mr. and Mrs. Frederick Moore (natives).
Sitka.—Rev. and Mrs. Alonzo E. Austin, Mr. and Mrs. U. P. Shull, Dr. B. K. Wilbur, Mrs. E. C. Heizer, Mrs. M. A. Saxman, Mrs. A. Carter, Mrs. L. S. Wallace, Miss A. J. Manning, Mrs. T. K. Paul (native), Mr. P. Solberg.
Fort Wrangell.—Rev. and Mrs. Clarence Thwing.
Jackson.—Rev. and Mrs. J. Loomis Gould, Mrs. A. R. McFarland.

Church of England.

Buxton.—Bishop and Mrs. Bompas, Rev. Frederick F. Flewelling, Miss MacDonald, Mr. R. J. Bowen.
Fort Selkirk.—Rev. and Mrs. B. Totty.
Rampart House.—Rev. and Mrs. H. A. Naylor, Rev. and Mrs. T. H. Canham.

Swedish Evangelical Mission Covenant of America.

Golovin Bay.—N. O. Hultberg, superintendent; Mrs. N. O. Hultberg, P. H. Anderson, school-teacher; Gabriel Adamson (native worker).
Unalaklik.—A. E. Karlson, superintendent; Mrs. A. E. Karlson, August Anderson, Miss Malvina Johnson, David Johnson, school-teachers; Miss Alice Omekejook (an Eskimo).
Yakutat.—K. J. Hendrikson, superintendent; Albin Johnson, Mrs. Albin Johnson, Miss Selma Peterson (at present in this country).
Kangekosook (outstation).—Stephan Ivanoff, assistant worker.
Kotzebue Sound (outstation).—Rock, a native evangelist.

GROUP OF ESKIMO BOYS. ST. LAWRENCE ISLAND, 1897. (See page 1005.)

Alaskan children in schools and families in the States.

Name.	Alaskan home.	Present location.
Robert Casey	Juneau	Haskell Institute, Lawrence, Kans.
Helen Kessler	Chilkat	Carrier Mills, Ill.
Edward Warren	do	Indian School, Chemawa, Oreg.
David Parker	Metlakahtla	Do.
Richard Smith	Jackson	Do.
Charles Hicks	Juneau	Do.
Amanda Brown	Sitka	New York City.
Katie Douglas	Metlakahtla	Newberg, Oreg.
Lydia Hanshaw	Hoonah	Do.
Louisa Ross	Juneau	Not known.
Archie Cameron		Sumner, Wash.
Minnie Baker		Parkville, Mo.
David and Fred Lewis		Washington.
Thomas Hanbury	Metlakahtla	Carlisle Indian School, Pennsylvania.
Joseph Flannery		Do.
Healy Wolf	Point Barrow	Do.
George Northrop	Sitka	Do.
Sidney Burr		Do
John Reinkin	Unalaska	Do
Samuel Kendall Paul	Sitka	Do.
Lablok		Do.
Oonaleana		Do.
Mary Moon	Chilkat	Do.
Susie Moon	do	Do.
Annie Reinkin	Unalaska	Do.
Dora Reinkin	do	Do.
Sospatra Suvoroff	do	Do.
Pelagia Tutikoff	do	Do.
Eudocia Sedeck		Do.
Mary Kedashan		Do.
Lottie Hilton	Juneau	Do.
Elizabeth Walker	Fort Wrangell	Do.
Jessie Annobuck		Do.
Annie Coogidlore		Do.
Ruth Eswetuck		Do.
Adelaia Kolilook		Do.
Nettie Toniecock		Do.

PRESBYTERIAN MISSIONS.

The Sitka Industrial School.—This largest of all the industrial schools in Alaska was established in 1880 by the Board of Home Missions of the Presbyterian Church. The buildings are admirably located on an elevation about 200 feet from highwater mark about midway between the town of Sitka and Indian River. An abundant supply of pure water is brought in pipes a distance of three-fourths of a mile. The water is forced to a height of 80 feet into a large tank by means of a force pump, and from this source all the buildings, including the hospital, are supplied. In connection with the school are eight "model cottages" where the married couples from the school begin housekeeping in "Boston style," as the natives express it. Funds for the erection of some of the cottages were loaned (without interest) by the Indian Rights Association; others were erected with money furnished by benevolent individuals in sympathy with this rational method of dealing with the Indian problem. The young people who occupy these cottages have a life lease of the ground, and are expected to pay for the cottages in installments. The average cost of a cottage is $350. We expect these model homes to be centers of purity, from which will radiate influences that will be far-reaching and lasting in their results. Here family life is established and family ties are held sacred; here industry, frugality, perseverance, and thrift are developed; here old heathen customs have no place—no Indian doctors, no witchcraft, no plural wives, no drinking, no gambling, no reckless living. In these homes the young husbands have a chance to develop into manly, self-respecting men and the young wives into tidy, industrious women.

Hospital.—In 1889 it became evident that a place was needed for the care of the sick, and Mrs. Elliott F. Shepard, of New York, very liberally donated the money for the erection of a hospital for the girls. Later a boys' hospital was erected near by. In 1892 it became evident that it was unwise to attempt to carry on two separate establishments, and the boys' hospital was somewhat enlarged and the upper floor devoted to a ward for girls. This combined hospital was opened for patients November 22, 1894. Previous to 1894 the building had been opened only to patients from the school, but now the wards were opened to natives from any part of

Alaska. The following is a summary of the work during 1897: Number of patients treated, 206; aggregate number of days in hospital, 2,594; average number of days, each patient, 12.5; number of prescriptions to in-patients, 2,634; percentage of deaths, 3; unimproved, 2; improved, 12; cured, 83. Causes of death: Tuberculosis, 3; capillary bronchitis, 3. Number of out-patients treated in doctor's office, 1,119; number of operations performed, in-patient, 38; total number of prescriptions made since June, 1894, 10,581.

Language.—The children speedily acquire an English-speaking vocabulary when strictly prohibited from using their native dialects. For five years English has been the exclusive language of the school. Experience has removed all doubt as to its expediency. The use of their vernaculars (Thlinget, Tsimpshean, Hydia) seriously retards their progress and does them no essential benefit. No schoolbooks have ever been printed in any of their native dialects. Each distinct people has a dialect of its own, local in character, and in course of time the vernacular dialects of the tribes of southeastern Alaska will become obsolete and English will everywhere prevail. As a matter of preservation the Society of Alaskan Natural History and Ethnology has lately commenced to reduce the Thlinget language to writing, which we hope to accomplish through the instrumentality of Mrs. Paul and Miss Willard.

Culinary department.—This department is a place of great interest to the pupils, both boys and girls, small and large. All want to come into the kitchen to work and to learn to cook. The boys wish to know how to cook good meals and bake good bread, pies, and cakes. They often ask if they can come into the kitchen to work, and this stirs up a spirit of emulation among the girls so that they beg to work in the kitchen; consequently, there is no lack of those who desire to work in these departments.

In the bakery the work is too heavy for the girls, and is done entirely by the boys. During the past year they have averaged 140 pounds of flour baked daily, turning out from 90 to 100 loaves of delicious bread a day. When the girls serve in the kitchen, they bake the pies and cakes and the boys in their turn do the same, which is during the winter season, that being the hard period of work. Much attention has been given to the quality of food, and in the past few years it has been greatly improved. One great victory won in the battle of work in these departments is cleanliness. In this direction there has been a vast improvement made. It is a pleasure now to be with them and hear them say: "Oh, this must be very clean; I want it to be clean and nice." Viewing these departments, they have made rapid progress in the last year.

The kitchen is supplied with both hot and cold water. The greatest obstacle in the work of these departments is the annoyance of having green wood much of the time.

The sewing room has been enlarged and nicely papered. The light is admitted from the east, so that they get the benefit of the morning sun. This department is well equipped, and the amount of work done each week is surprising. The girls over 7 years of age knit their own stockings. In the sewing department they learn quickly and accomplish much. Sewing machines are in daily use, and the girls soon learn to use them. Almost every graduate has a machine of her own.

All the shoes are made by the boys, apprenticed under the direction of a master workman. Considerable custom work is also done.

Gardening.—Mr. John Gamble, gardener and general worker, has three medium-sized plats of arable land. One garden, which has been cultivated for several years, produces lettuce, beets, peas, and onions in abundance. Of the other gardens, which are new, one is planted in potatoes and the other sown in turnips. Cereals, for lack of warmth and sunshine, do not ripen. Currants, rhubarb, raspberries, cauliflower, and celery are easily grown. Fruits, such as apples, plums, and pears, have not been fully tested, but it is believed that they could be grown with success.

Blacksmithing can hardly be classed among the trades by which a man can earn a living in Alaska, yet there is much work in this line, doing repairs about the mission, mending machinery, repairing stoves, making stovepipes and camp hooks, sharpening tools, and doing miscellaneous jobs for the citizens of the quaint little capital. Soldering and a little tin work are also done. The constant wear and tear in most of the work departments require much repairing, nearly all of which is done by the boys.

Painting.—Two or three of the boys have received instruction in this useful branch of industry, and are kept busy painting, papering, glazing, and calcimining.

Recreations and amusements.—The home life of the school is particularly pleasant. Their games and plays are such as white children enjoy, consisting of games of marbles, baseball, townball, playing soldier, flying kites, sailing ships, target practice with bow and arrow, authors, checkers, dominoes, rope jumping, hide-and-seek. Coasting and skating are indulged in by both sexes. Then there is an organ for the girls and another for the boys, and violins, guitars, fifes, bugles, and the irrepressible mouth organs are among the amusements and recreations of each day.

A rational system of discipline is easily and well maintained. Those in charge aim to make the industrial training school just what its name implies. Manual occupations are in reach of the pupils as fast as they acquire sufficient knowledge of the English language to enable them to prosecute the learning of a trade with success. To accomplish anything permanent and of material benefit in the way of mastering trades they must first acquire a fair, common-school education, before which they are not prepared to serve an intelligent apprenticeship. After certain initiatory advancement has been made, industrial training is then made coequal with schoolroom work. While the boys are taught trades, the girls are taught all branches of household industry. Indeed, the appointments and work of the school are such as to familiarize them with American ways of living and to ingraft into their lives industrious habits.

The steam laundry, with its labor-saving machinery, relieves the teachers and pupils of much hard drudging work incident to a school of this character, where water and soap must be used in such copious quantities.

Carpentry department.—All of the buildings on the mission premises, twenty or more, have been built by boys apprenticed to this trade, under the supervision of a competent foreman. Shopwork consists in the making of furniture, bookcases, clothespresses, screens, chests, curtain poles, picture frames, hand sleds, bric-a-brac work, and undertaking. The outdoor work consists of joining, framing, contracting, and building. Sailmaking and boat building are among the useful industries of this department. Among our carpenter apprentices a number have shown special aptitude as artists and designers. The spirit of earnest industry is most praiseworthy, and the boys appreciate their opportunities.

In the winter of 1887–88 the Society of Alaskan Natural History and Ethnology was organized and incorporated. The purpose is to collect and preserve in connection with the Sitka Industrial and Training School specimens of the natural history and ethnology of Alaska.

In addition to the Sitka Industrial School, the Presbyterian Board of Home Missions maintains stations at Point Barrow, St. Lawrence Island, Haines, Hoonah, Juneau, Fort Wrangell, and Jackson.

MORAVIAN MISSIONS.

We are indebted to the Rev. J. Taylor Hamilton, secretary of the Moravian Society for the Propagation of the Gospel, for the following sketch of the progress of Moravian mission work in Alaska:

Moravian missionary and educational work in Alaska began in 1884, at the suggestion of Dr. Sheldon Jackson. After a preliminary tour of exploration, the then practically unknown region of the Kuskoquim and Nushagak rivers was selected. To establish the work two ordained missionaries, the Revs. William Weinland and John Kilbuck, were sent out with their wives, together with a lay assistant, Mr. Hans Torgersen, who was to superintend the erection of the needful houses. Mr. Kilbuck is a full-blooded Indian, the descendant of a long line of distinguished Delaware Christians, and, like his colleague, was a graduate of the Moravian College and Theological Seminary at Bethlehem. Before one house had been erected Mr. Torgersen was accidentally drowned in the Kuskoquim River. Before any converts had been won Mr. Weinland and his family had to withdraw, owing to seriously impaired health, later to labor in California. For a while Kilbuck and his wife held out alone, contending with the severities of a climate which in winter sometimes reached 60° of cold below zero, and with the difficulties of the Eskimo language. But God blessed their zeal and fidelity. The first sign of any reward for their labor was given on Good Friday, 1887. In the best Eskimo at their command the missionaries had been striving to acquaint the people with the love of God, and now he was telling that the blood of Jesus Christ cleanseth from all sin, when an old Eskimo interrupted him: "Thanks. We, too, want our badness washed away."

From the inception of the mission attention has been paid to education, and at the three main stations—Bethel and Ougavig, on the Kuskoquim, and Carmel, on the Nushagak—industrial schools have been steadily maintained, except when for brief intervals lack of provisions, after a season of failure in the catch of salmon, has compelled a temporary intermission. The schools at Bethel and at Carmel are boarding schools; that at Ougavig a day school. The two former during certain years in the past have been Government contract schools. Two boys were for a period entered at the Government school at Carlisle, Pa., and are now serving as assistant missionaries. The pupils at Bethel average about 30, at Carmel 35, and at Ougavig 15.

At present 15 missionaries are in this field. On the staff are a graduate of the Hahnemann Medical College, Philadelphia—Dr. Herman Romig—and two professional nurses. Four hundred and seventy patients were cared for at Bethel during the last year, for which a report has been received. Three principal stations are occupied and seven outposts. Twenty-seven native assistants cooperate in the care of 625 converts, young and old. On January 30, 1897, the first fruits of home mission work among the Eskimos themselves were gathered in the baptism of a convert at a village 80 miles from Bethel, up to that time served by two native assistant missionaries. For several years the mission at Bethel has had a steam sawmill in operation, the natives bringing logs and receiving planks in exchange. It is hoped that thus decent houses will gradually supplant the underground hovels of a former time.

When the missionaries came they found the Eskimos filthy, degraded, cruel, the prey of the medicine men or shamans, given over to superstition, seeing evil spirits in everything, without knowledge of God and without hope for the future. In the reeking atmosphere of their underground kashimas, 16 to 24 feet square, three or four families, two to three dozen persons, might cower over the fat lamps. Privacy and decency were unknown. The standard of morality was utterly low. The aged and the sick were taken out and exposed to death by cold or starvation, lest a kashima should become haunted by death occurring within. The persons of the people swarmed with vermin. Now the decencies of family life and the proprieties of civilization are beginning to be prized. Heathen rites have practically ceased through a considerable stretch of country.

That the Eskimo will ever become civilized in a mode patterned after that of the European or American is scarcely to be expected. Climatic conditions and environment are against this. But it is hoped he will imitate the culture and civilization of the Laplanders. The Moravian mission is, therefore, deeply interested in the success of the effort to distribute the domesticated reindeer throughout Alaska, the benevolent project with which Dr. Sheldon Jackson is so closely identified. This is desired, both as a civilizing medium and as likely to afford a more assured means of subsistence than the precarious products of the chase and the uncertain returns of toil on the waters. But it is also earnestly desired as likely to afford a more regular and frequent means of communication and transportation. At present an exchange of letters between the mission and its schools on the one hand and the church at home on the other can be counted upon with certainty only once a year.

CONGREGATIONAL MISSIONS.

The Rev. C. J. Ryder, corresponding secretary of the American Missionary Association of the Congregational Church, has prepared the following statement with regard to the work of the society at Cape Prince of Wales:

This station is under the care of the American Missionary Association, the society of the Congregational churches. Work at this station was begun in 1890.

Geographically.—Cape Prince of Wales is situated on the most western point of mainland in the United States, only a few miles from the Arctic Circle. The country is broken and mountainous running back from the shore of Bering Strait. Much driftwood is available here and is utilized by the missionaries in the erection of their cottages. The station holds a good position strategically for reaching the Eskimo in the interior of Alaska. The Eskimo residents at Cape Prince of Wales are especially active and energetic for people of this race. They are counted among the great smugglers of the North. In former reports in this Bureau reference has been made to this fact. From Cape Prince of Wales the natives cross the straits and carry on trade in " deer skins and sinew and wooden ware of Alaska," which they exchange for walrus, ivory, skins of tame reindeer, and whale blubber of Siberia." They also secure in this way " firearms and whisky," neither of which prove very important factors in their Christian civilization.

Missionary force.—Messrs. W. T. Lopp and H. R. Thornton were the first missionaries in this field. They opened the work at Cape Prince of Wales in 1890. Two frame buildings were erected. One of these was occupied as their home and the other was used for school and chapel purposes. These buildings are still standing. Mr. Thornton was murdered August 19, 1893. His murder was committed by some native desperadoes who were soon after punished by the Eskimos themselves. His death did not indicate any opposition on the part of the natives generally to the work. Mr. Lopp and his wife have continued work in the field until the present, and are still there. Mr. Lopp has proved very efficient in his administration. He has been commissioned by the United States Government to conduct important investigation along the coast to the north of Bering Strait. He has also had charge of the reindeer herd assigned by the Government to this station, and has been commissioned to go to the north upon an expedition to relieve the whalers that are locked in the ice.

Present condition of the station.—From the last reports received by the American Missionary Association we gather the following facts concerning the present condition of the work at Cape Prince of Wales. Mr. Lopp had been absent in the States for some months and was most cordially received by the natives upon his return. He entered immediately upon preparation for the winter. Driftwood for fuel and building purposes was rafted down the coast, which was a considerable undertaking. Mr. Lopp reports to the American Missionary Association as follows:

A log house 22 by 24 was finished and divided into kitchen, two bedrooms, a storeroom, and hall. During the winter the house is buried in snowdrifts to the roof, making our side windows almost useless. Two sides and roof were sodded, a sod lean-to 20 by 12 was built onto the front in October, which is used as a vestibule, woodhouse, and carpenter shop. This temporary inclosure, or entrance as we call it, was lighted by sky-windows, made of clear blocks of ice. This house has proved decidedly the most comfortable and convenient house we have ever used in the Arctics. A house for herders was built near ours. It is the same style as ours and has been used as a home for them when in from the camp. It is hoped that these two buildings will prove object lessons which will not be lost to this settlement. A house which they can use both winter and summer, a compromise between their underground and the civilized house, is undoubtedly what they need.

"Mr. Thornton's monument, which was purchased in San Francisco with funds contributed by Southport, Conn., friends, gave these natives a much needed object lesson in respecting the dead. Before taking the monument up to the grave, we exhibited it at a Sunday service in the Storrs Chapel, explaining to the people its object. We also told them about visiting Mrs. Thornton and her little son and the kind words of greeting which she sent to them and the prayerful interest which she had in them all.

"To think of Mr. Thornton lying in an Arctic grave recalled to us that he often expressed a sentiment so similar to that of the African missionary who is said to have compared pioneer mission work to building the foundation for a great bridge, and, God willing, was content to lie in an African grave as one of the unseen foundation stones.

"A big Christmas box sent by Dr. Storrs's missionary boys (may their tribe increase), containing knit caps, nuts, pocketknives, beads, dolls, etc., a box of ship biscuit contributed by Mrs. Thornton, and dates and raisins from our own supplies on Christmas made it a memorable day—Christmas, 1896.

"Since 1894 no prizes have been given for attendance at school. One serious objection to the prize (biscuit) system was that it educated them to think we were under obligation to them for attending school.

"*The religious work.*—Two sermons have been preached almost every Sunday. The Sunday school had an average attendance of more than 100 during the winter months. Having but four teachers, the classes were often large. We hope some of the advanced pupils will soon be able to take classes. It was very gratifying and sometimes amusing to see the interest taken in the collection boxes every Sunday. Lead, powder, caps, cartridges, spoons, matches, muskrat, ermine, and squirrel skins were contributed. We expect to use this collection to build a small mission house in the neighboring settlement where driftwood is plentiful.

"*Reindeer herd.*—The mission herd of reindeer has passed successfully through the three winters and now numbers about 360. It has been free from diseases which have afflicted seriously the Government herd at Port Clarence. To milk a cow they lasso her and throw her to the ground. The milk has no unfavorable or distasteful flavor and is highly prized by us who have had to depend upon the 'tin cow' so many years. The herders live in deerskin tents. Our herders consist of six Eskimos. With but $54 worth of goods and supplies, it required close managing to feed and clothe nine people one year. These six herders should have been permitted to devote their entire time to herding, driving, and breaking, but the limited amount of supplies compelled us to use one or two in turns at the Cape to hunt and work. With our nets and rifles we got some white whale, seals, and fish, and in June walruses, which kept them fairly supplied. Each of them now owns between 35 and 45 deer and we hope in a year or two, when they can live independent of mission support, that the influence which they will exert as Christian deermen will do much toward leading the natives along this coast 'out of darkness into light.' What a pleasure when visiting in camp to see them bow their heads and offer thanks to God before eating; to lead them in a little prayer meeting where every one joins and to sing with them 'A tent or a cottage, why should I care?' Go-ten-um, who is about 21, is considered the best deerman. He is of a mechanical turn of mind and made the wood cuts for the Eskimo Bulletin. A trip on reindeer sleds with Kiv-yearz-ruk through the mountains to Port Clarence was made in January. While there we had an opportunity to visit the Government herd, talk with the Laplanders, and assist in two services on Sunday, which were well attended. Our people have not prospered as in previous winters. A threatened epidemic in the fall together with the 'hoodoos' which followed, partly accounted for this. Distilling and drunkenness throughout the year often prevented many from making the most of a favorable wind. The walrus season has not been favorable, but at this writing they have all well filled meat houses. We rejoice that the reindeer herd will give a livelihood to the people for the next few years, and this influence may be far-reaching. In conclusion, we wish to thank our many friends for their kind letters and their prayerful interest in this work. We feel especially grateful to the few churches and persons who have shown by their gifts that they believed that these poor Eskimos were included in Matthew xxviii, 19. Surely none can be more in need of the gospel than these. With this burden upon our hearts, we pray God that in the future this mission may receive the support which we think its importance deserves."

BAPTIST MISSIONS.

Mrs. James McWhinnie, superintendent of the Alaska Work of the Woman's American Baptist Home Mission Society, sends the following account of the society's work on Wood Island:

In 1884 it was decided that the Baptists should establish a mission in Alaska. From Mount St. Elias to the Shumagin Islands, with Kadiak as headquarters, was set aside as Baptist ground.

September 22, 1886, marks the beginning of Baptist missions in Alaska. From that time until 1890 the work was done by teachers appointed and supported by the Government and commissioned by the American Baptist Home Mission Society. Mr. and Mrs. W. E. Roscoe, Mr. and Mrs. J. A. Wirth (supported in part by Dr. Jackson and friends in Seattle), and Mr. and Mrs. Faodorf were at different times Government teachers. These all advocated the establishment of an orphanage as the true way of doing missionary work in Alaska.

This work was undertaken by the Woman's American Baptist Home Mission Society of New England. The frame of a building was purchased and forwarded to Alaska in the summer of 1892. In March, 1893, Mr. W. E. Roscoe was sent by the society to the territory to select location and conduct the work.

July 4, 1893, the first child was received into the orphanage. For two years Mr. Roscoe labored earnestly in the development of the work, during which time 24 children received their care in the home.

In the summer of 1893 Miss Carrie Currant was sent as teacher, but was compelled to return in November on account of ill health. In September, 1894, Miss Lulu C. Goodchild arrived as reenforcement, and continued with the work until her marriage, July, 1897. Mr. Roscoe having resigned to return to the States, Mr. and Mrs. C. P. Coe were appointed to take charge, and arrived on the field June 5, 1895. In the following September Miss Hattie B. Snow was added to the force of workers, but was compelled by broken health to return to her home in August, 1897.

Mr. and Mrs. Coe found 18 children in the home. Since that time 14 have been added.

These children have been received upon different conditions. Some have been apprenticed by their parents to the mission until they become of age; others—waifs—have been apprenticed by the United States commissioner; others still are received from parents who pay a nominal charge for their care.

The boys are taught gardening, use of tools, care of stock, etc. They cut the trees for wood, saw and chop them up for use, carry water, fish and hunt. The girls are taught to wash, iron, scrub, sew, bake, cook, mend, and care for the house.

Religious services are held every day, and in these the children take great interest and enjoyment. They sing and recite Scripture, and make the services largely their own.

Miss M. E. Mellor, Teacher, and Pupils, Unalaska.

EDUCATION IN ALASKA.

In the past year and a half several improvements that add much to the value and appearance of the premises have been added. First was built a woodshed 20 by 30 feet, for storing and cutting wood, with rooms above for play rooms, shop, and storage—a very essential improvement when we consider the number of rainy days for which Alaska is noted. Next followed a cottage, situated at a distance of about two minutes' walk from the orphanage. Last, but more important than the others, came the chapel. It contains one room 26 feet square, one 12 by 20 feet, and a tower 8 feet square. The whole was completed at a cost of $600. The Woman's American Baptist Home Mission Society paid one half, the other half being raised on Wood Island, or sent by friends for that purpose. The North American Commercial Company, which does business on this island, furnished the labor gratis.

July 26, 1896, the Wood Island Baptist Church was organized with six members. Since that time one, the oldest girl of the orphanage, has been added by baptism.

The day school is open to the children of the native villagers. Last year, notwithstanding the opposition of the priest, 21 of them were enrolled. For the past two winters night school also has been held for the benefit of young men and youths. The attendance was gratifying.

Last year it was Mr. Coe's privilege, during the summer, to preach to the people at Kadiak every other Sunday. The services were appreciated and would have been renewed this summer, but, being the only man on the place, demands on him for manual labor made it impossible to do so. The society has already voted to employ an industrial teacher, and after he is secured, there will be more time for outside missionary work. The cost of our present work is estimated at $4,500 annually.

METHODIST MISSIONS.

The Jesse Lee Home, Unalaska.—In September the home was able to be removed from the rented building, which it had occupied for several years, into new and commodious quarters of its own. The building is the admiration of all residents. It is a large, two-and-a-half-story building, and with the exception of the Government schoolhouse is the most pretentious building in the place. It is in charge of two Methodist ladies, Miss Agnes L. Sowle, of Hagaman, N. Y., being principal, and Miss Sarah J. Rinch, of Canada, being her assistant. Residing under the same roof and giving some assistance outside of school hours are the sisters Misses Elizabeth and Ada Mellor, who teach the Government school.

There are at the present time 30 children in the home belonging to the Aleut race. During the last summer one of the girls in the home was taken at the expense of a wealthy citizen of Chicago to that city to be educated, and three or four others were sent to Captain Pratt's celebrated school at Carlisle, Pa.

The school is doing a large preparatory work for that people. If in the near future there shall be any native teachers in the Aleutian Islands, if there shall be any native Christian homes and native Christian parents, they are now in process of being created by that school—the Jesse Lee Memorial Home at Unalaska being the only evangelizing influence at work among the Aleuts of Alaska.

When in November the revenue cutter *Bear* was ordered to the Arctic Ocean to try and land a relief party to go overland to the 400 whalers imprisoned in the ice and in danger of starvation, north of Point Barrow, Captain Tuttle announced through the newspapers of Seattle that he would be very glad to carry free of freight any Christmas presents that the citizens might wish to send to Unalaska for the destitute Aleut children and the children in the Methodist Home. The project was taken up with enthusiasm by the teachers in the public schools of that city, and the children in those schools made Christmas presents to the children in Unalaska. To the surprise of every one, about two tons of dolls drums, whistles, jumping jacks, games, picture books, candy, etc., were sent in, so that the friends of the mission had the satisfaction of knowing that Chrismas was to be a very happy day at that distant mission.

Unalaska Harbor being the natural stopping place for vessels passing from Seattle or San Francisco to the Yukon River, has grown into new importance through the gold discoveries, so much so that this present winter six iron steamers are being built in its harbor, employing some two or three hundred white workman, and there ought to be a Methodist minister stationed there that these men as well as the natives might have gospel privileges.

The coming and going of so many sailors make it very important that a hospital should be established at that place, which could be very appropriately done in connection with the Methodist mission work.

THE SWEDISH MISSION COVENANT'S MISSIONS IN ALASKA.

The Rev. D. Nyvall contributes the following account of the operations of the society at Yakutat, Unalaklik, and Golovin Bay:

The mission work, now carried on in Alaska by the Swedish Mission Covenant of America, was begun by the Mission Covenant of Sweden. It was at the annual conference in Stockholm in 1886 that the Swedish Covenant decided to begin its mission among the heathen people in Alaska. They then sent out Mr. A. E. Karlson and Mr. Adolph Lydell to begin missions among the Alaskans.

On the 25th of June, 1887, Mr. Karlson arrived at St. Michaels, in northern Alaska, where, owing to the lack of necessary communications, he had to remain a whole year before he could return to the United States to procure the necessary supplies. In the summer of 1888 he returned to San Francisco to procure materials for a house and other necessaries.

Mr. Lydell stopped at Yakutat, south of Mount St. Elias. As soon as he had determined on the location of his station he went to San Francisco to secure supplies and provisions, returning to Yakutat in 1888, accompanied by Karl John Henrikson, whom he by a special providence of God had accidentally met in Oregon. Lydell, however, was taken sick immediately after his return to Yakutat. Having suffered from a severe pulmonary affection, he was not able to continue his missionary work in those cold regions. On the advice of physicians he went back to California, and in his stead Mr. Albin Johnson was sent out in 1889. As soon as Mr. Lydell's health permitted he took up the work of a traveling missionary in the United States, in which work he has since engaged. His work consists in traveling among the mission friends to arouse an interest for the Alaska mission and to solicit means for the same. In this he has succeeded well. The interest manifested in this country for this mission is to a great extent due to the work of Mr. Lydell.

At first the missionaries met only with adversities and obstacles. It was not an easy task in this cold country to get a home to live in. They succeeded, however, in getting some boards, but not sufficient for a house; hence they were compelled to go into the woods, fell the trees, and split them with an ax into boards and shingles. This was hard work; but they succeeded. They arranged in the newly made home first a large room for public gatherings, and even before it was finished they assembled the natives in the kitchen and preached to them by means of an interpreter.

From the United States money was plentifully contributed, with which the missionaries built a children's home in Yakutat. The building was a two-story house, containing room for the missionaries, room for the children, and a large schoolroom, which also served as a church. In this house twenty-four children were educated. In short, the skies of the future appeared almost cloudless.

Suddenly there came an unexpected stroke as a thunderbolt from a clear sky. On the 8th of January, 1892, the home was suddenly burned down, and with it nearly all the property of the mission, together with that of the missionaries, was destroyed.

At about the same time that this calamity took place a good step was taken toward success. A steam saw had been received the fall before. Henrikson had bought this saw with money subscribed for the purpose through the efforts of Mr. Lydell. The saw was not yet in working order, but everything was ready for its erection when the home burned. When the home had burned and all the books and material for the school had been destroyed, the missionaries got time to devote themselves to the erection of the sawmill. This mill was built of logs cut in the woods and split with the ax into boards. As all of their blankets and clothing with which they paid the natives had burned, they resolved to do all the work without any assistance from them. This, however, they were not allowed to do. Said the natives, "Permit us to work; we will ask no pay. We will eat at home, and if you get anything in the future you can repay us." With their aid the work made rapid progress, so the sawmill was in running order by the time the first boat arrived in the spring.

The result of the work of the sawmill was that the entire village was rebuilt. It was converted from a number of poor shanties to neat and comfortable lumber houses, built along streets, as in our towns. This change took place within a couple of years.

At present there is a congregation at Yakutat of 38 persons who have received the Christian baptism. This congregation is organized in accordance with the same principles of our mission congregations in Sweden and America and hold their services in the same manner. There is even a Young People's Society, organized with the purpose of joining the young in their work for their Master. This society

EDUCATION IN ALASKA.

has proved a great help to the young against the temptations to attend the dances and festivities of the heathen.

Knowing what a powerful factor a Christian school is, it is encouraging to learn that from 60 to 100 children are educated in the mission school. Although the home has not been rebuilt, yet five children are reared and educated at the station. The property at this station is valued at $3,570.

In the spring of 1891 Miss Hannan Sevenson, from Worcester, was sent out to superintend the children's home at Unalaklik. Mr. David Johnson, of Harcourt, Iowa, who has been called as school teacher at Unalaklik, went out in her company.

To the credit of the people it must be said that it has been very quiet and peaceful in this community. Drinking parties and rows are seldom heard of. At Christmas time and during the week of prayer many were touched by the Holy Spirit. We had a full house every evening. The natives sang, prayed, and testified. Even a young Shuman arose and said that he should not like to be left when the Lord would come.

At the mission station six boys and three girls have been supported. They are all obedient, and live for God.

In the spring of 1892, Mr. August Anderson, in company with one of the boys at the school, made a missionary tour along the western coast. They then came to Golovin Bay, where Anderson found many Eskimos in poverty and darkness. He asked the natives if they wished to have a school in which their children could learn about God. They all answered "Yes."

Mr. Anderson returned home to Unalaklik and told his brethren what he had heard and seen. It was in the summer of this year that Mr. Karlson started on his tour through the United States and Sweden. Having reached the States, Mr. Karlson began to collect money for the mission at Golovin Bay, receiving at his first meeting, which was held in San Francisco, a collection of $70 as a beginning. Arriving at Rockford, Ill., when the Covenant's annual meeting was in session, he put forth his cause orally as well as in a written report. This exerted such an influence on the whole meeting that immediately, at the same session, about $1,500 was raised for the Alaska mission among the delegates. Subscriptions continued at the general meetings until the sum was increased to $3,000. We all, who were present, remember what a missionary spirit prevailed at this blessed meeting.

The following summer, when Karlson returned to Alaska, he had in his company Mr. N. O. Hultberg and Miss Malvina Johnson. Golovin Bay was assigned to Brother Hultberg as his mission field, and he went there directly from St. Michaels on the boat which brought up Mr. Karlson. There he met his coworker, Mr. August Anderson. They now first had an earnest prayer meeting, after which they took up their work with zeal. They got along so well in building their house that they could assemble the people during the very same fall. They kept up their meetings during the winter.

The following spring they had the joy of baptizing several natives. The following fall Brother Hultberg left Golovin Bay to assist in the work at Unalaklik, and so Mr. Anderson was left alone at Golovin Bay. In the spring Mr. Hultberg made his way down to St. Michaels to meet his betrothed. Their wedding took place at Unalaklik. The fourth day after their marriage the newly wedded couple went to Golovin Bay, where they since have labored.

We have now in that place a mission house, dwelling house, and a schoolhouse, and, better than all, a congregation of Christians numbering 35 members. Forty children attend the school, and 4 are supported at the Children's Home. The mission property at this station is valued at $2,525. This sum does not include the value of the 160 acres of land, which, according to the laws of the United States, belong to the station.

The members of the congregation at Unalaklik number 40. The school children number between 60 and 70. Four children are supported at the Children's Home. The property is valued at $4,490.

MISSIONS OF THE PROTESTANT EPISCOPAL CHURCH.

In the Terrritory of Alaska this church has work among the whites at Juneau and Douglas and Sitka, and among the Indians of the Yukon region and the Eskimo of arctic Alaska, all under the supervision of Bishop P. T. Rowe. The following extract is taken from the annual report of the board of managers of the Domestic and Foreign Missionary Society of the Protestant Episcopal Church: "The Rev. Mr. Prevost, whose station at Fort Adams is among the Indians, the bishop temporarily removed to Circle City, as it was the more important for the moment and a convenient center. In June last the Rev. Mr. Chapman, who, with his faithful wife and Miss Sabine, is stationed at Anvik, 600 miles from the mouth of the Yukon, wrote home that the mission school at that place, though unable to care for more than two or three boarding pupils, had a most prosperous year. In November, and again in December, Mr. Chapman visited the villages upon the Chageluk Slough, to the eastward from Anvik. He hopes to establish a school there with a native teacher. In April Mr. Chapman made a visit up the Kuskokwim River as far as Vinisahle."

From Point Hope Dr. Driggs, under date of June 7, reports that on his return to duty from a visit to the States he received a joyful and hearty welcome from the natives on his arrival at Point Hope. The Doctor has erected a new home for himself at this place, in the building of which natives and a few white men assisted. The interest in the Sunday services has been very marked, the average attendance being 120 and 125. A widespread epidemic of influenza made its appearance during the summer. The outlook here is very encouraging, and Dr. Driggs says: "I doubt if there is a single city or village in the United States where the ratio to the population of those who attend worship on Sundays has been as large the past winter as it has been here at Point Hope."

The statistics last reported are as follows: Stations, Anvik (10 communicants); Circle City, Indian Mission; Fort Adams (3 communicants); Nowikowkat, Fort Yukon (5 communicants); Point Hope. Mr. Prevost reports large numbers of baptized Indians within his district. Number of missionaries, 8.

STATEMENT WITH REGARD TO MR. DUNCAN'S WORK AMONG THE TSIMPSHEEAN INDIANS OF BRITISH AMERICA AND ALASKA.

On the 1st of October, 1857, Mr. William Duncan, of England, arrived at Fort Simpson, British Columbia, to open a mission among the Tsimpsheeans. He found by actual count that they numbered 2,300. They were barbarians of the lowest type, and their history little less than a chapter of crime and misery.

On the 28th of June, 1858, he had so far acquired a knowledge of the language that he was able to open his first school in the house of a chief, with an attendance of 26 children and 15 adults.

In April, 1860, he made preaching tours to the various villages situated on the rivers which empty into the ocean near Fort Simpson.

Having secured a few followers among the natives, he proposed to them that they remove from the native village, where they were more or less under the influence of their heathen neighbors, and establish a new village that should be under strict regulations. The removal was accomplished on the 27th of May, 1860, the people arriving at their new location, 16 miles south of Fort Simpson, the next day at 2 o'clock. There were 50 men, women, and children, that composed this first colony. On the 6th of June 290 additional natives joined them. Every one desiring to settle in the new village was required to subscribe to the following agreement:

1. To give up sorcery.
2. To cease calling in sorcerers when sick.
3. To cease gambling.
4. To cease giving away their property for display.
5. To cease painting their faces.
6. To cease drinking intoxicating liquors.
7. To observe the Sabbath.
8. To attend religious instruction.
9. To send their children to school.
10. To be cleanly.
11. To be industrious.
12. To be peaceful.
13. To be liberal and honest in trade.
14. To build neat houses.
15. To pay the village tax.

The new village, notwithstanding the above stringent regulations, grew very rapidly until it had a population of 1,000 natives. They had erected for themselves good, comfortable frame houses; had a steam sawmill, a salmon-canning establishment, and a village store owned largely by native shareholders. A number of them had learned the carpentry trade, others furniture making, and still others boat building and boot and shoe making and the various industries in villages.

Their prosperity continued until about 1880, when the news of the remarkable success of the mission had circulated wherever the English language was known.

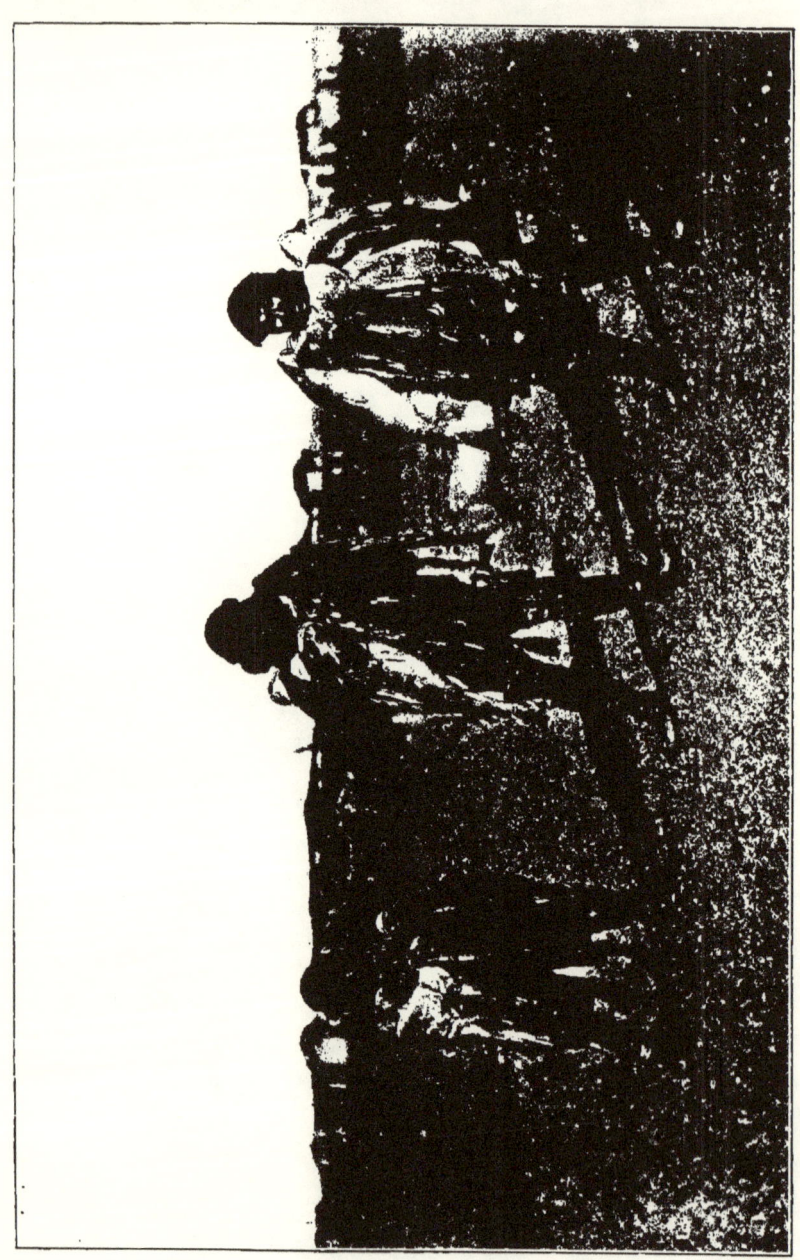

NATIVES WITH CODFISH. ST. LAWRENCE ISLAND, AUGUST, 1897. (Page 1605.)
By V. C. Gambell.

This had attracted a great deal of attention to the mission, so much so that the Church of England, whose missionary society had originally sent Mr. Duncan to the field, thought that the importance of the mission demanded a bishop and one was selected, ordained, and sent. The coming of the bishop to the station immediately started rivalries. If the bishop was to be at the head of the mission, Mr. Duncan, who had given his life to the work and had created the mission, would have to take a second place, which he could not very well afford to do. On the other hand, the bishop could not afford to allow Mr. Duncan to rule and he himself take a second place.

In the meantime the attention of the Canadian Pacific Railway authorities had been attracted to the increasing importance of Northern British Columbia and Alaska, and they had sent surveyors for a preliminary survey, with regard to running a mail road to the coast at that point. When the people found that the railroad surveyors were driving stakes over the lands that they and their fathers had occupied for generations, they protested. Finding that their protests were of no avail, they sent a committee to Ottawa to lay their grievances before the Canadian Parliament, Securing no redress there, the committee continued their journey to London, but were prevented from having a personal interview with the Queen, and returned home very much discouraged. Upon agitating the question of their personal rights, they found that they had no right whatever to the land that they had always supposed to be their own, and that there was no future for their children, under the regulations provided by the Parliament of British Columbia. This, in connection with the land difficulties and the difficulties of the church combined, made them very much dissatisfied; and finally, in the winter of 1886-87, they sent their leader, Mr. Duncan, to Washington, to confer with the President. Secretary of the Interior, and leading officials of our Government. the result of which was that in the spring of 1887 they concluded to leave British Columbia and move in a body to the contiguous Territory of Alaska, in the United States. They supposed, of course, that they would be allowed to take down the houses which they owned, and transport their windows, doors, lumber, etc., over to their new home, which was about 60 miles north of the old place. They were, however, disappointed in this, as an official of the British Columbia Government forbade their taking anything. And this people, that had slowly come up from barbarians to civilization, were compelled to go out empty-handed, leaving behind them all the property which they had accumulated during those nearly thirty years that they had been emerging from barbarism to civilization.

On the 7th of August, Mr. Duncan returned from Washington and landed at Port Chester, on Annette Island, the place that had been selected for their new home. It was a great gala day for the people. A United States flag, donated to them by the ladies of Philadelphia, in Independence Hall, was flung to the breeze with cheers and firing of guns. Addresses were made by Mr. Duncan and several tourists who were with him on the steamer. A prayer for God's blessing followed, and the public exercises were closed by the people singing with great ardor the doxology, "Praise God from whom all blessings flow."

The timber was cleared off a number of acres for a village, which was duly surveyed and plotted and allotted to the inhabitants. A steam sawmill and a large store building were erected. Friends in Brooklyn, New York, and other cities sent several thousand dollars for public improvements. Since then a large schoolhouse, church, and salmon cannery have been erected.

Congress, in section 15 of the act entitled "An act to repeal timber-culture laws, and for other purposes," approved March 3, 1891 (26 Stats., 1095), has reserved Annette Island for the colony. Section 15 of the above-mentioned act reads as follows:

"Until otherwise provided by law, the body of lands known as Annette Island, situated in the Alexander Archipelago, in southeastern Alaska, on the north side of Dixon's entrance, be, and the same is hereby, set apart as a reservation for the use of the Metlakahtla Indians and these people known as Metlakahtlans who have recently emigrated from British Columbia to Alaska and such other Alaskan natives as may join them, to be held and used by them in common, under such rules and regulations and subject to such restrictions as may [be] prescribed from time to time by the Secretary of the Interior."

In British Columbia they have formed a local government, which they transferred with themselves to their settlement on Annette Island. This local government is officially known by them as "The Town and Associated Community of Metlakahtla," An annual election is held by the members of the "community." This council makes the laws, and is the governing power of the people. Every person desiring to unite with the community is required to make application to the "council" for membership. If the request is granted, the new member subscribes to the following rules, which have superseded those in force when the colony was organized:

We, the people of Metlakahtla, Alaska, in order to secure to ourselves and our posterity the blessings of a Christian home, do severally subscribe to the following rules for the regulation of our conduct and town affairs:

1. To reverence the Sabbath and to refrain from all unnecessary secular work on that day; to attend divine worship; to take the Bible for our rule of faith; to regard all true Christians as our brethren, and to be truthful, honest, and industrious.
2. To be faithful and loyal to the Government and laws of the United States.
3. To render our votes when called upon for the election of the town council, and to promptly obey the by-laws and orders imposed by the said council.
4. To attend to the education of our children and keep them at school as regularly as possible.
5. To totally abstain from all intoxicants and gambling, and never attend heathen festivities or countenance heathen customs in surrounding villages.
6. To strictly carry out all sanitary regulations necessary for the health of the town.
7. To identify ourselves with the progress of the settlement, and to utilize the land we hold.
8. Never to alienate, give away, or sell our land or building lots or any portion thereof to any person or persons who have not subscribed to these rules. ―――― ――――.

(Signed) ―――― ――――.
―――― ――――, witness.
Date, ―――― ――――, 189—.

Already before migrating to Annette Island Mr. Duncan had introduced these elements of civilization. Many of his tribe were individual owners of the village lots occupied by their residences and vegetable gardens. Immediately after removing to Annette Island the same plan of individual ownership was resorted to in the form indicated by the following certificate of ownership:

Certificate No. —.   Dated ――――.

METLAKAHTLA.

This certifies that ―――― ―――― has this day, in pursuance of the rules and regulations of the Town and Associated Community of Metlakahtla, Alaska, entered upon and occupied that certain tract or parcel of land on Annette Island, in the district of Alaska, U. S. A., more particularly described as follows, viz: ――――, and is now in the actual possession thereof.

That, so far as this city and associated community can confer such a privilege, he has, and ―――― heirs shall have, the prior and exclusive right of proving up ―――― claim thereto, and of obtaining title from the United States Government, and this shall be the evidence thereof, except it be before us canceled upon our register for abandonment or conduct unbecoming an American citizen.

Done by our order, under our seal, the day and year first above written, by the chairman and secretary of our native council.

[SEAL.]
By ―――― ――――,
Chairman of the Native Council.
And ―――― ――――,
Secretary of the Native Council.

The island is about 40 miles long by 3 wide. The colony on Annette Island have cleared off the timber from their village site, erected from 150 to 200 good frame residences, established a cooperative store, salmon cannery, and steam sawmill, and built a large church; but, so far as known to this office, nothing has been actually done in mining, although it is known that projects in this direction have been under consideration by them. All the industries are carried on by the native people themselves, under the leadership of Mr. William Duncan.

INTRODUCTION OF DOMESTIC REINDEER INTO ALASKA.

The progress has been satisfactory and an advance has been made during the year.

While no purchases have been made in Siberia, 466 deer have been added to the herds by birth, making a total on June 30, 1897, of 1,466. A new station has been established about 60 miles north of St. Michael, Norton Sound. This location is on the north shore of Unalaklik River, about 10 miles above its mouth, and combines a central position, with dry and abundant pasturage, good fishing, timber for building and fuel, with easy access to the ocean. The new station is central for the distribution of the herds either northward to Kotzebue Sound, Point Hope, and Point Barrow; southward to the Roman Catholic and Moravian stations on the Lower Yukon, Kuskokwim, and Nushagak rivers, or eastward to the Episcopal stations and mining settlements on the Upper Yukon Valley, being about the same distance from Bering Straits on the west, Point Barrow upon the north, the Middle Yukon Valley on the east, and the Kuskokwim Valley on the south. Located in the neighborhood of the leading mission stations among the native populations, it will be able to draw and educate as herders and teamsters a larger number of the native young men.

At the Teller Reindeer Station no additional buildings have been erected or were needed during the year. Three sod houses 16 by 10 feet in size lined with lumber were erected at the winter quarters for 1896-97 on the Agheeopak River for shelter of herders and their families. Several smaller sod huts were erected at various places between the Teller Station and Agheeopak as a refuge for the herders while en route to and from the station. A few log dwellings and store houses will this winter be erected at the new station on the Unalaklik River. The buildings at the Teller Station, with furniture, boats, sleds, harness, nets, and other property of the Government, are in good repair.

PERSONNEL.

Mr. William A. Kjellmann, who resigned the position of superintendent in the fall of 1895, having expressed a willingness to again enter the service, was reappointed to his former position as superintendent.

A. N. Kittilsen, M. D., of Stoughton, Wis., was likewise appointed assistant superintendent and physician, and the Rev. T. L. Brevig continued as teacher.

Herders.—The Lapps continue to justify the wisdom of their importation from Lapland, embodying in their own training and skill the knowledge and methods learned by their people through centuries of experience and observation. Their services in Alaska are invaluable.

In the introduction of reindeer into Alaska and the training of native men in their management and care it is important that that training should be in accordance with the latest and most improved methods of handling reindeer; that the Lapps possess these above all other nationalities is universally recognized. Their assistance has proved so valuable and is so essential to the immediate future that Mr. Kjellmann has gone with your consent to Lapland this winter to secure and bring over a permanent colony of them. The Lapps now in Alaska were brought over with the understanding that they would be returned at the end of three years; this was the best arrangement that could be made at the time. The limit of service being reached, Messrs. Rist, Somby, Kemi, and Eira. with their families, have returned to Lapland. Messrs. Tornensis, Nakkila, and Larsen have been prevailed upon to remain, with the expectation that they will become herd owners and permanent citizens.

During the winter of 1896-97 Messrs. Rist and Nakkila were detailed to accompany the superintendent on his sledge journey to the Yukon and Kuskokwim valleys. Mr. Aslak L. Somby remained in charge of the herds at Golovin Bay until March, when he returned to the Teller Station and was sent to the Cape Nome herd to relieve Mr. M. A. Eira, whose wife needed the medical attendance of the station physician.

Mr. Frederick Larsen was detailed for a month's service with the herd at Cape Prince of Wales. Messrs. Tornensis and Kemi had charge of the Teller Station herd, except as one or the other made short trips with the physician.

Apprentices.—The school of apprentices consists of the same persons as last year—five married and two unmarried Eskimos. They have shown an alacrity in work, a faithful adherence to instructions, and an effort to understand all parts of the work that augurs well for their future success.

Rations.—During the year a change has been made in the rations, decreasing the amount of American food (such as flour and meats brought from the outside) and increasing the amount of native food (such as fish, seal, and oil).

School.—As the herders and apprentices have been with the herd 60 miles away from the station much of the time, the school has been mostly composed of Eskimo children, resident in the immediate vicinity of the station. Although debarred regular schooling, both the Lapps and apprentices are slowly acquiring the English tongue. The superintendent recommends that some of the young people be given a few years at school in the States to learn English.

Sickness.—Dr. Kittilsen, the physician, has attended to 60 cases of sickness among the employees or their families and 250 cases among the outside Eskimos, who have in some cases come 200 miles on a dog sled to secure medical attendance. There was but one fatal case at the station, being Mrs. Eira, who remained too long at Cape Nome before applying for help. She passed to her rest May 4, 1897.

HERD.

On the 1st of July, 1897, there were in Alaska 1,466 head of domestic reindeer. These are divided into four herds, and located as follows:

Government herd at Teller Reindeer Station	525
Congregational herd at Cape Prince of Wales	367
An undivided herd at Golovin Bay controlled jointly by the Swede and Episcopalian Missions	296
Herd in charge of the Eskimos at Cape Nome	278
Total	1,466

The Government herd was wintered on the Agheepak River 20 miles from its mouth.

In the spring it was driven to the south side of Eaton River as a more favorable place for fawning, and this summer has been kept on the south side of Port Clarence in the neighborhood of Cape Riley.

Fawning.—There were born at the Teller Station 149 living fawns, at Cape Prince of Wales 124, at Golovin Bay 108, and at Cape Nome 85, making an increase for the year of 466.

Sickness.—In the fall of 1895, and again in the fall of 1896, a disease broke out in the herd similar to foot-rot in sheep. With a change of the herd to drier ground the sickness gradually abated.

Breaking.—Special attention has been given to the training of the reindeer both to harness and the pack saddle. During last winter 46 two and three year old deer were thus broken. This makes 73 well broken and trained sled deer in the Government herd. In the herd at Golovin Bay are 18 sled deer, and at Cape Prince of Wales 22.

At the Teller Station the sled deer were kept in constant practice, both on their own account and also for the training of the Eskimo apprentices. Including the trip to the Kuskokwim Valley the aggregate number of miles driven was over 10,000.

This practice will be kept up, preparatory to their introduction into the mining camps for freighting and traveling.

REINDEER FREIGHTING.

The first incentive to the introduction of domestic reindeer into Alaska came as an act of humanity to provide a new food supply for the Eskimos, who were subject to periodical seasons of starvation, their old food supply of whale, walrus, and wild animals having been partially destroyed by the greed of white men. But since the discovery of gold mines in subarctic Alaska and the consequent influx of thousands of miners, it has been found that the reindeer is as essential to the white man as to the Eskimo.

The first thought of the miner in central Alaska is to secure a good "claim;" his next thought is the question of "food supply"—whether he can secure provisions that will enable him to work his claim continuously, or whether for the want of such provisions he will be compelled to leave his claim unworked a portion of the year while he goes where he can secure food—not only losing the profit that would accrue from the claim if worked, but also involving him in heavy traveling expenses in going to and fro.

With the exception of fish, a little wild game, and a limited quantity of garden vegetables, there is no food in the country. All breadstuffs, vegetables, fruits, and the larger portion of the meat supply must be brought into the country from the outside. A small quantity of provisions is packed on sleds and on men's shoulders and brought over the passes in the Chilkat country of southeast Alaska to the head waters of the Yukon; there barges or flatboats are built, and with their freight are floated down the Yukon River to the neighborhood of the mines. The great bulk of the food supply, however, is brought in on steamers plying on the Yukon River. These provisions are necessarily left in warehouses on the banks of the great river. But the miners, who are the consumers, need them at their claims, which are from 10 to 100 miles away from the river. Now, it should be remembered that there are no roads in Alaska as they exist in other sections of the United States; and, with the almost illimitable area of bog and swamp and tundra and frozen subsoil, it will be impossible to make and maintain roads, except at a cost that would be practically prohibitive.

In summer the supplies are loaded into small boats, which are poled up the small streams or packed on men's backs to the mines. In winter they are hauled on dog sleds. This costs heavily. From Circle City to the Birch Creek mines, a distance of about 50 miles, the freight is 10 cents a pound ($200 a ton) in winter and 40 cents in summer ($800 a ton). From Dawson to the Klondike mines, a distance of 15 miles, the freight last winter was 8 cents a pound ($160 a ton), and this summer 25 cents, or $500 a ton of freight 15 miles. In addition to the expense, the carrying capacity is too limited. A load is from 100 to 125 pounds on a sled per dog, a portion of which is food for the dogs, and if the route is a long one, without intervening sources of supply, they can not carry more food than is sufficient for themselves. So far they have failed in supplying the mines with a sufficient stock of provisions.

Last winter the steamer *Bella* was caught in the ice and frozen up at Fort Yukon, 80 miles distant from Circle City. An effort was made to forward the provisions with dog teams on the ice, but it was a failure. The food could not be moved in sufficient quantities and with sufficient speed to supply the miners of the Upper Yukon, and by spring at Dawson City flour ran up to over $100 per barrel, $50 to $125 per 100 pounds.

A few horses have been brought into the country, but in the absence of roads, scarcity of food, and rigor of winter climate they have not proved a success. At Dawson, although the wages of a man and team are $50 a day, yet even that does not pay, with hay at $125 to $150 per ton (and not a pound to be had when I was there in July even at those figures), and the horses fed on bread made from flour ranging in price from $100 to $200 per barrel.

The only solution of the question of reasonable land transportation and rapid communication and travel between mining centers hundreds of miles apart in subarctic Alaska is the introduction and utilizing of domestic reindeer.

The reindeer is to the far north what the camel is to desert regions, the animal which God has provided and adapted for the peculiar, special conditions which exist. The greater the degree of cold, the better the reindeer thrives. Last winter a party of them hauling nine sleds made a day's journey with the temperature at 73° below zero. On a long journey through an uninhabited country a dog team can not haul sufficient provisions to feed themselves. A deer, with 200 pounds on the sled, can travel up and down the mountains and over the plains without a road or trail from one end of Alaska to the other, living on the moss found in the country where he travels. In the four months' travel of 2,000 miles last winter the deer were turned out at night to find their own provisions, except upon a stretch of the Yukon Valley below Anvik, a distance of 40 miles. The great mining interests of central Alaska can not realize their fullest development until the domestic reindeer are introduced in sufficient numbers to do the work of supplying the miners with provisions and freight and giving the miner speedy communication with the outside world. It now takes from fifty to sixty days to carry the mail between Juneau and Circle City. With the establishment of relay stations at suitable distances the reindeer teams will carry the same mail in four or five days.

The reindeer is equally important to the prospector. Prospecting at a distance from the base of supplies is now impossible. The prospector can go only as far as the 100 pounds of provisions, blankets, and tools will last him, and then he must return. With ten head of reindeer, packing 100 pounds each, making half a ton of supplies, he can be gone for months, penetrating regions hundreds of miles distant, his deer grazing wherever night finds him. The possibilities are so great, that in the days to come it will be a matter of surprise that the utilization of the deer was not vigorously pushed at the start.

SIBERIAN PURCHASE STATION.

In 1892 the introduction of domestic reindeer into Alaska was undertaken to provide a new food supply for the Eskimo. The new demand that has now arisen to assist the miners in the opening of the country emphasizes the imperative need of some method of procuring the deer from Siberia in larger numbers. To assist in this, last winter permission was secured from the Russian Government at St. Petersburg, through the regular official channels, for the United States to locate an agent at some suitable point on the coast of Siberia for the continuous purchase of reindeer through the year. Hitherto the work of purchasing has been confined to five or six weeks in summer.

By extending the time for purchasing through the whole year it is hoped to be able to secure a large number and have them on the coast ready for transportation during the short summer, when Bering Sea and the adjacent arctic coast are free from ice. Mr. John W. Kelly, who has spent years in arctic Alaska and is familiar with the conditions of the country, was appointed agent. Associated with him are Conrad Siem and Mr. A. St. Leger, both of whom have had years of experience with the natives of the Arctic.

A good opportunity offering, Conrad Siem took passage on the whaler *Bonanza* May 29. Mr. Kelly, with supplies and stock of barter goods, sailed from San Francisco June 9 on the schooner *Volant*, reaching St. Lawrence Bay, Siberia, on July 17, three days after the arrival of Mr. Siem.

When the needs of the reindeer for domestication and transportation are met, early steps should be taken to stock the larger islands of Alaska, especially those in Bering Sea and along the Aleutian group.

In Dr. G. Hartwig's Polar World, page 89, it is stated that "In the year 1770 thirteen reindeer were brought into Iceland from Norway. Ten died on the passage, but the three which survived have multiplied so fast that large herds now (1869) roam over the uninhabited wastes. During the winter, when hunger drives them into the lower districts, they are frequently shot, but no attempts have been made to tame them."

A WINTER TRIP OF 2,000 MILES.

Since the commencement of the herd in 1892 the obstacles that it was predicted would prevent the successful introduction of domestic reindeer into Alaska have either been proved to be groundless or have one by one been met and overcome. Having shown by actual experience that they could be bought, transported, and successfully propagated, it remained to give a practical demonstration of their ability to traverse any part of the country under the most unfavorable circumstances and with a temperature at times lower than experienced by some of the Arctic expeditions.

This was done last winter, in accordance with your directions. At 3 p. m. on the 10th of December, 1896, with the temperature at 15° below zero, Mr. William A. Kjellmann, the superintendent, accompanied by the Lapps Per Aslaksen Rist and Mikkel J. Nakkila, started from the Teller Station with 9 sleds and 17 head of reindeer to demonstrate the capacity of the hardy and swift animal for winter travel in Alaska. Native trails and well-known sections of country were ignored, to show their ability to go anywhere. The course, while traveled by compass, was a zigzag one, in order to better learn the extent and abundance of moss pasturage. Scaling high mountain ranges, shooting down precipitous declivities with tobogganing speed, plodding through valleys filled with deeply drifted snow, laboriously cutting a way through the man-high underbrush of the forest, or steering across the trackless tundra, never before trodden by the foot of white man; gliding over the hard-crusted snow, or wading through slush 2 feet deep on imperfectly frozen rivers unknown to geographers, were the experiences of the trip.

The second day of the journey, with the temperature 43° below zero, and over a rough, broken, and pathless country, they made a distance of 60 miles.

After celebrating Christmas with Rev. Mr. Hultberg and the Swedish missionaries on Golovin Bay, December 30 found Mr. Kjellmann's party crossing Norton Sound, an arm of Bering Sea, and getting into a crevasse filled with snow, from which they escaped without much damage.

The next day, keeping on the ice along the coast, hummocks were found so steep that steps had to be cut up and over them to enable the deer to cross.

On New Year's day, coming to a flagstaff projecting from a huge snow bank, they found under it, completely buried in the snow, the comfortable home of the Rev. Mr. Karlsen and the Swedish missionaries at Unalaklik. On the afternoon of January 11 and morning of the 12th, 85 miles were made in twelve hours. The native guides at St. Michael being afraid to undertake a winter trip across the country to Ikogmute, the Russian mission on the Yukon River, and affirming that it could not be done, Mr. Kjellmann started on January 19 without them, traveling by compass.

On the 23d, while crossing a barren mountain range, they were overtaken by that dread specter of arctic regions, a Russian poorga.[1] Neither man nor beast could stand against the blast. The reindeer were blown down and the loaded sleds overturned. The men, throwing themselves flat, clung to one another and to mother earth to keep from being blown away. Stones and pieces of crushed ice flew by, darkening the air. A lull coming toward evening, with great difficulty a little coffee was made, after which the storm broke with renewed fury during a night which to the travelers, clinging to the earth with desperation,

---

[1] An arctic blizzard.

TCHUTCHEE GIRL.
By J. W. Kelly.

seemed endless. The following day a belt of timber was reached and rest and safety secured. January 25 and 26 found them cutting a way for the deer and sleds through a dense forest, from which they finally emerged to wade through snow and water 2 feet deep and the temperature at zero. On the 31st they encountered a succession of driving, blinding snowstorms while crossing the tundra south of the Yukon delta, being reduced to such straits that they were compelled to cut the railing from their sleds for fuel. On February 5 the storm passed away, leaving the temperature at 73° below zero, causing even the reindeer to break loose from their tethers and tramp ceaselessly around the tents for warmth.

Notwithstanding the severe cold the journey was continued, and at 2 o'clock in the afternoon they found shelter and a warm welcome from the Moravian missionaries at Bethel. On the 10th of March, between the Kuskokwim and Yukon rivers, a lake 15 miles wide was crossed.

The struggle for life commenced, however, on the 11th, when they reached the Yukon, and, contrary to information, found no moss for the deer. A push was made up the Yukon to reach, if possible, the Episcopal mission at Anvik. There being no food, the march was kept up all night, plowing their way through loose snow from 2 to 4 feet deep, and on through the 12th with snow falling fast. That afternoon two of the deer fell dead and were left with their sleds where they fell, while the journey continued uninterruptedly through the blinding snow the second night. On the 13th two more deer dropped dead and were abandoned, as the party with desperate energy pushed ahead day and night for food and life. On the 14th another deer fell in his traces. That evening a native hut was reached and the continuous march of four days and three nights without sleep or rest and without food for the deer was over. Trees were cut down by the Lapps that the deer might browse on the black moss that hung from them, while Mr. Kjellmann, suffering with a high fever, was put to bed by the medicine woman, and dosed with tea made from some medicinal bark. On the 17th one of the Lapps, who had been scouring the country, reported moss upon a mountain 60 miles away. The deer were unharnessed and driven to the distant pasturage, while Mr. Kjellmann continued his journey to Anvik on skis. In the hospitable home of Rev. Mr. Chapman he was nursed back to health and strength.

The return journey to the Teller Station was made without any special adventure, except, on the 16th of April, getting into a crack in the ice while crossing Norton Sound and soaking the load with salt water. On the 24th of April the Teller Station was safely reached after a trip of 2,000 miles, the longest ever recorded in any land as made by the same reindeer.

The result of this trial trip has convinced missionaries, miners, traders, and others residing in northern and central Alaska that domestic reindeer can do for them what they have been doing for centuries in Lapland. That when introduced in sufficient numbers they will supplant dogs, both for traveling and freighting, furnish a rapid means of communication between widely separated communities, and render possible the full and profitable development of the rich mineral interests.

A TRIP UP THE YUKON.

During July and August, through the courtesy of the North American Trading and Transportation Company, I was able to take Mr. William A. Kjellmann and make a trip of 1,600 miles up the Yukon River. This trip was made to secure for you the information you sought with regard to the adaptation of the country for reindeer and the special conditions which will meet the introduction of reindeer freighting. The results of the trip were satisfactory, and I returned more than ever deeply impressed that the great pressing need of the hour is more reindeer and more Lapps.

BRANDING.

As year by year increasing numbers of reindeer are passing into the ownership of the apprentices and missions, and as others are looking forward to ownership in the near future, it is important that rules should be formulated for the regulation and registering of brands that mark such ownership.

ITINERARY.

Leaving Washington on the 1st of June last, I embarked at Seattle on the steamship *Portland*, of the North American Transportation and Trading Company, on the 12th, reaching Unalaska, Dutch Harbor, on the 21st. Two days were spent at Unalaska visiting the school and attending to school matters.

At 5.30 a. m. on the 23d our steamship sailed for St. Michael. On the 25th we reached the ice and all day skirted the ice floe, reaching St. Michael at 1 o'clock on the morning of the 27th.

On the 28th the Yukon River steamer *Portus B. Weare* arrived, having on board a large number of miners with half a million dollars' worth of gold dust from Klondike and the Yukon mines. It was the arrival of this steamer with its treasure on July 17, 1897, at Seattle that aroused the attention of the world.

The 29th was signalized by the arrival of the cutter *Bear*, Capt. Francis Tuttle in command. The *Bear* had on its upward trip called at St. Lawrence Island, St. Lawrence Bay, Cape Prince of Wales, and Teller Reindeer Station, bringing favorable reports from the several stations; it also brought to St. Michael Mr. William A. Kjellman, superintendent of the Reindeer Station, whom I wished to accompany me on a trip upon the Yukon River Valley, that he might investigate the supply of reindeer moss and ascertain the conditions that must be met in the establishment of future reindeer freighting establishments from the provision warehouses on the river back to the interior mines.

On the 3d of July I transferred from the ocean steamship *Portland* to the river steamer *Portus B. Weare*, and on the morning of the 5th we left the wharf at St. Michael for the mouth of the Yukon River. Owing to the great quantities of silt brought down in the waters of the Yukon, Bering Sea has so shoaled that ocean steamers at present are unable to reach nearer the mouth of the river than St. Michael, which is 60 miles north of the river, on the coast of Bering Sea.

At 10 o'clock the steamer reached Pastolik, where a stop was made to take on firewood. Half an hour later we entered the north pass of the delta and at 11.30 went aground on the bar, where we lay for twenty-four hours, until lifted off by the tide. Although there was a cold, drizzling rain, a number of the passengers went on shore to hunt geese and ducks, which are plentiful at that season of the year. At high tide, July 6, the steamer again floated, and, taking on wood near Kutlik, we started up the river.

The Yukon is one of the great rivers of the world. Taking its rise in the mountains of the Northwest Territory of Canada, it flows across the entire width of Alaska from east to west, dividing that great Territory into two nearly equal parts. Its delta stretches for 20 miles along the sea and extends 100 miles inland, a distance so great that, standing upon one shore of the delta, the table-lands bordering the other can not be seen. This great delta is comparable to that of the Mississippi River in the accumulated silt of years, which greatly extends the area of the land into the sea, shoaling the navigable waters of the sea to such an extent that ocean vessels bound for St. Michael are compelled, while passing the mouth of the river, to make a detour to the westward. Through its whole course the river, like the Missouri, carries a large amount of sediment in its waters, and the extent of its deposits upon its delta will not be wondered at after the observer has traversed its length and seen a thousand miles of banks undermined and ready to be swept away.

Like the McKenzie River of Canada and the Lena of Siberia, which rise in the south and flow northward, the Yukon feels the influence of the warmer temperature of spring first at its source. The ice brought down by the strong freshets of the Upper Yukon is piled upon the firm unbroken ice of the lower stream, with the result of accumulating great masses of ice and water until the weight of the ice and the increased pressure of the gathered waters force out a section of the bank. This process is repeated again and again lower down the river. The breaking up of the ice on the Yukon is one of the grand sights of earth, rivaling in interest the remarkable auroras of the winter months in that northern latitude. Upon such occasions, great masses of ice from 8 to 10 feet thick are hurled with Titanic force into the river banks, gouging out yards of soil and uprooting great trees before their momentum is checked. Thus unceasingly through the centuries this great stream goes on leveling down the hills of central Alaska, picking up the soil and carrying it in solution hundreds of miles to the coast, and it is deposited where the fresh water meets the salt of the sea. The trees thus carried out to sea are nature's provision for the Eskimos on the treeless coast of Bering Sea and the Arctic Ocean, driftwood being their only fuel. This vast delta region of the Yukon is filled with marshes and lakes and is liable to overflows; it is also a breeding ground of innumerable wild geese and other fowl.

The river is navigable for light-draft steamers for 2,000 miles to Fort Selkirk and even beyond that point, with short portages around rapids, while its tributaries—the Anvik, Koyukuk, Tanana, Porcupine, White, Pelly, and other rivers—are navigable for from 100 to 600 miles.

A middle-aged lady who was following her husband to live in this wilderness was so impressed with the continuous steaming up this great river day and night, week after week for three weeks, without passing a single large town, and only seeing small Indian settlements, or here and there a fishing camp or trader's post, while the great yellow flood seemed to flow on with but little diminution in volume, that she felt as if she had been on the river for ages, and broke out with the exclamation, "Will it never come to an end; must I continue to go on and on for ever and ever?" and retiring to her stateroom found relief in a good cry.

At 5 a. m. on July 7 the steamer reached the head of the delta, where another supply of firewood was taken on board. Indeed, during the whole trip the steamer seemed to stop about every six hours for wood. The river is lined with white pine, which is cut by the natives and piled up convenient for the steamers. This wood costs from $4 to $6 per cord, and the steamer uses from 25 to 30 cords a day. Leaving the head of the delta, low hills begin to appear along the north bank of the river. For 300 miles farther the river was so wide that in places, standing upon one bank, the other could not be seen.

At 8.30 a. m. we reached Andreafski, 216 miles from St. Michael, where we stopped for wood, and also for mending our boiler pipes, which were leaking badly. At this village were several well-hewn log houses, back of which were a number of graves, the dead being deposited in boxes laid on top of the ground. All central and northern Alaska, including the Yukon Valley, has a frozen subsoil which never thaws out. This has been dug into 30 feet without getting below the frost. On the banks of some of the streams north of the Yukon a stratum of frozen soil has been found over 100 feet thick. Yet to look upon the acres of brilliant wild flowers and of grasses waist high, and miles upon miles of white pine, aspen, and willows, with the thermometer above 100° in the shade, it is very difficult to realize that one is under the Arctic Circle.

Owing to the difficulty and almost impossibility of digging graves in the frozen ground with rude native implements, the custom universally prevails of depositing the dead in boxes either on the ground or on platforms above the reach of wild animals.

At Andreafski we first met the birch-bark canoe, showing that this village was on the border land between the Eskimos of the coast and the Indians of the Interior, the universal boat of the Eskimos being the skin-covered kiak and that of the Indian the birch-bark canoe. Andreafski has secured some prominence this season as the point to which provision supplies from St. Michael that could not be taken to the mines on the upper courses of the river were landed for winter use, and also to be accessible to the river steamers in the early spring, the ice in the Yukon River breaking sometimes a month in advance of the ice in Bering Sea. This permits the river steamers to load up in the spring and go to the head waters of the river and return down the stream to the coast by the time that ocean steamers can reach St. Michael through the ice of Bering Sea.

The low shoals which were encountered at the ocean side of the delta gradually increase in size as the river is ascended until at the head of the delta they become islands, upon which poplars and willows are found 20 to 30 feet high.

Soon after leaving Andreafski, scattered white pine began to appear. Leaving Andreafski and rounding a bold promontory, we passed the mouth of Andreafski River, a broad stream flowing from the north and passing through a gold-bearing country. Two miners were reported as having been seen on the stream some months working mines.

At 9 a. m. on July 8 we reached Ikogmute, or, as it is more popularly known, the Russian Mission. It has a population of 150 natives, and is 315 miles by way of the river from St. Michael. At this place Father Belkoff, the former priest of the Oriental Greek Church (now an invalid) built one of the best church buildings belonging to that denomination in Alaska. Father Orloff, the present priest, has an excellent garden on the hill slope in the rear of the parsonage. Just above the village, bold and perpendicular rock cliffs save the village from being swept away by the great yellow floods which sweep along their base, or ice gorges which form each spring in its vicinity. Along the entire village front were racks covered with salmon hung up to dry for the winter. The run of salmon this season has proved very large. A year ago the run of fish was correspondingly poor, and as a result last winter there was great scarcity of food among the people. One woman and a boy actually starved to death.

At 2 o'clock in the morning of July 9 the steamer reached Koserefski (410 miles). This is the location of the largest mission of the Roman Catholic Church on the Yukon River. A number of passengers remained up to visit the mission, but upon going to the buildings found everything securely locked, and the teachers so soundly asleep that they were unaware of the presence of the steamer.

After breakfast the steamer reached Anvik (457 miles), where we remained three-quarters of an hour to get wood for the steamer. On shore, chained to posts, were from twelve to fifteen sled dogs belonging to the villagers. These dogs are found in every settlement and fishing camp in Alaska. They are a cross between the dog and the wolf, receiving but little attention from their owners. When not upon their journey they subsist chiefly by foraging and become adept thieves, so that everything eatable, even their own harness, has to be stored away on platforms above their reach. This has given rise to the custom everywhere prevailing along the Yukon River and in northern and central Alaska of erecting small log houses upon platforms elevated 10 or 12 feet above the ground. These houses are used for storing dried fish and other property that needs to be kept beyond the reach of the dogs. Among other things, these dogs are celebrated for their habit of howling at night. Upon the approach of a stranger some dog will set up a howl, upon which all the dogs within hearing will join in. There may not be over a dozen dogs in the neighborhood, but when they commence to howl a stranger would be sure that there were a hundred, if not a thousand, of them.

These dogs are the common carriers of Alaska, dragging sleds in winter and carrying packs in summer. The average load of a dog sled is 125 pounds. The great drawback to their use is the necessity of carrying food for them on long journeys. A team of dogs carrying freight requires a second team of dogs for hauling food for the two teams, and when a journey is required through an unsettled section of the country dogs become unavailable because of the impossibility of carrying sufficient food or procuring fresh supplies for the teams. This difficulty will be overcome when domestic reindeer are introduced into Alaska in sufficient numbers to dispense with the use of dogs. The reindeer will haul heavier loads and cover greater distances than the dogs and require no transportation of food for its own maintenance. When the day's work is done they can be turned out to graze, even in the severest weather of the winter. The reindeer is to the arctic and subarctic regions what the camel is to the oriental and tropical lands.

Anvik is the first of a series of missions of the Protestant Episcopal Church. The missionaries at this point are the Rev. and Mrs. J. W. Chapman and Miss B. Sabine. Mr. Chapman has, under great difficulties, erected a neat little chapel, a comfortable residence, schoolrooms, and boarding house for the shelter of the Indian children taken into the home. A small sawmill has also been erected in connection with the mission.

From the mouth of the river to its source, through all the vast Yukon Valley with its tributaries—indeed all over central and northern Alaska—mosquitoes abound in July and August in such numbers as to become a veritable plague. The hot sun of summer thawing the frozen ground for a few inches leaves water standing, unable to soak away through the frozen subsoil beneath, converting the whole country into one immense swamp, from which are bred clouds of mosquitoes. They are so great an infliction that some of the teachers declare that the extreme cold of winter (77° below zero) is preferable to the mosquito time in summer, and strong, vigorous men accustomed to hardships have been known to sit down on the ground and cry like children under the torture of mosquitoes. While the river steamers are in motion the passengers are not much troubled with them, but when a landing is made for putting on freight or taking on wood the mosquitoes swarm aboard in quantities, compelling the use of netting for the protection of the head and face and of leather gloves for the hands. Wild animals sometimes die from the effects of their stings.

On Saturday, July 10, while "wooding up," the passengers picked wild currants just turning red. They also found protruding from the bank of the river ice, which was brought on board. We were now at a point where in winter the natives are accustomed to portage across the country to Unalaklik and thence down the coast to St. Michael. From St. Michael by way of the river is 550 miles, across the portage about 150 miles, making a saving in distance of 400 miles.

At midnight we reached Nulato (648 miles). This village is in the neighborhood of the most remote of the early Russian trading posts, which was established by Nalakoff in 1838, after which he and his party returned to St. Michael for the winter. During the winter the buildings were burned by the natives.

In 1841 the post was reestablished and rebuilt by Deravin. In 1851 it was the scene of a massacre, among the victims being Lieutenant Barnard, of the British navy, and a member of Admiral Kollinson's expedition in search of Sir John Franklin. Lieutenant Barnard had been detailed to ascend the Yukon River and ascertain whether the natives could give any tidings of Sir John Franklin's party. Reaching Nulato, he dispatched one of the employees of the fur company and an Indian into the Koyukok Valley for information. The Russian, on his arrival at the native village, fell asleep on his sledge, and in the absence of his servant, who had gone to obtain water, was killed by the natives, the servant himself being afterwards killed. The murderers then gathered a force of about one hundred and started for the Russian post at Nulato. Reaching a settlement of the Nulato

Indians, they heaped wood, broken canoes, paddles, and snowshoes in front of the entrance and smoke holes of the native houses, and then, setting them on fire, suffocated almost the entire population, only five or six escaping. The next morning, swarming into the courtyard of the fort, they made an attack, killing the commander, also Lieutenant Barnard and others. No punishment was ever meted out to the murderers, and the reason of their wholesale butchery remains involved in mystery.

This village is the site of a Roman Catholic mission, and Father Monroe, the priest, was at the landing to greet us. At Nulato the Yukon River, which has been running for 350 miles in a northern and eastern direction, turns directly eastward. Just above the village is the mouth of the Koyukuk River, a large tributary from the north. A small steamer has ascended this river some 600 miles, and gold has been found along its course in paying quantities. I gathered from the fur traders that have been in the country for many years, and also from the miners that have been longest in the country, their conviction that when the gold fields of the country are explored and more is known concerning them, the richest mines in all Alaska will be found along the course of this stream. It is a noticeable fact that the tributaries of the Yukon flowing from the north are clear water, while those from the south are muddy like the main river. This is due to the fact that the streams from the south take their rise from the glaciers of southern Alaska, and also that some of them run through a region covered with volcanic ash, which is easily washed away and held in solution. In recent geological times there has been an eruption of volcanic dust in southern Alaska which has covered an area of 20,000 square miles to a varying depth of from a few inches to 50 feet.

On Monday, July 12, we passed, in the afternoon, the abandoned buildings of the old Tanana trading post, and a few miles farther on made a call at Fort Adams, the site of the St. James Episcopal mission. The missionaries in charge are Rev. and Mrs. J. L. Prevost. A pleasant call was had with the missionaries. Mrs. Prevost had the pleasure of having with her for a visit her mother from the East.

The Tanana trading post having been removed 8 miles from its former position to a point on the north bank abreast of the mouth of the Tanana River, the St. James Episcopal mission is also to be removed to the same neighborhood, the waters of the Yukon having shoaled and made a landing difficult at the old sites. The mouth of the Tanana, 897 miles from St. Michael, bids fair to prove a central and permanent location in the affairs of the Yukon Valley, being midway between the mouth of the river on Bering Sea and the crossing of the international boundary line on the Upper Yukon. This point has been recommended to the United States Government by Captain Ray, U. S. A., as the best location for a military post. If the Territory shall be divided into two districts, this point will probably be the capital of the second. It will also probably be the northern terminus of a trunk line of a railway either from Cooks Inlet or Prince William Sound, the railroad ascending to the Sushitna River to the head waters of the Tanana and down the Tanana to the Yukon.

On the 1st of March a meteor fell near the Episcopal buildings. Though the night was dark, the whole heavens were lighted up with its brilliancy. Many of the natives were much frightened at the phenomenon. During the past winter Ivan, the great chief of the Tanana, died and was buried in the mission cemetery. His kingdom stretched from Camp Stevens to Novikakat, on the Yukon River; also for 500 miles up the Tanana Valley and across the portage, including the head waters of the Kuskokwim River. From his early manhood he had proven himself the friend of the Russians, and latterly of the Americans. Many years ago the wife of a Russian trader who had a store in the Tanana Valley had incurred the enmity of some of the people, and one of their number was persuaded by the shamans to kill her, which he did by shooting her in her own house. Encouraged by the deed, arrangements were commenced for killing the trader also. At this juncture Ivan reached the scene and interposed to save the life of the trader. This so incensed the shamans that they threatened to kill him also. Drawing himself up to his full height of 6 feet, with flashing eyes he bade them defiance and saved the white man.

The natives of this region are in transition from their own to the white man's way. Old customs are losing their hold upon them, and it is doubtful whether any other leader will arise from among them.

At Nuklukahyet (Mayo's Place at the mouth of the Tanana) a miner was brought on board who had been found by the natives in a starving condition. He had been off prospecting by himself on the Koyukuk River. In running a rapid he lost his footing and all his provisions, saving only his gun and ax. His team of dogs were stung to death by mosquitoes. He struggled across the country for 300 miles, his only food a moose which he had shot and on which he had lived eighteen days. When found he was naked, starving, and out of his mind.

The Tanana is the largest of the tributaries of the Yukon. Taking its rise among the group of ice-covered mountains in southern Alaska, it flows northward, emptying into the Yukon. It is navigable for several hundred miles from its mouth. Gold has been found along its course. It has a scattered native population of about 1,000, who are under the care of the St. James Episcopal mission. The head waters of the Tanana rise on the high table lands from which also flow the head waters of the Sushitna and Copper rivers into the Pacific Ocean; the Forty Mile Creek and White River into the Upper Yukon. While the steamer lay at the mouth of the Tanana, taking on wood and cleaning its boilers, we received a visit from the Rev. J. L. Prevost on his little steam launch, the *Northern Light*. This vessel, 40 by 25 feet in size, was built by the Union Iron Works of San Francisco, and equipped with a Roberts safety water tube. It is capable of carrying a wood supply sufficient for forty-eight hours continuous steaming, and is fitted up with a comfortable cabin for the missionaries. This little launch has proved of great service in visiting the small native settlements on the Yukon and Tanana river, with their smaller tributaries. Mr. Prevost has the honor of publishing the first newspaper ever printed in the Yukon Valley. His little paper, called the Yukon Press, is practically an annual, but one number being published during last year. This paper, with the Eskimo Bulletin, also an annual, published at Cape Prince of Wales, Bering Straits, by W. T. Lopp, the missionary, are the only papers up to this time that have been published in central or arctic Alaska. As the editors of these Alaskan papers have had but one mail a year, it is not to be expected that their papers should appear any oftener.

On the afternoon of July 13 the steamer entered a section of the Yukon Valley known as "Lower Rampart." This was formed by the river in some former age having broken through a range of mountains. The scenery through the canyon was so grand and wild that but few of the passengers were willing to go to bed, but remained up nearly all night.

Early in the morning of July 19 we reached the mouth of Munook Creek (1,075 miles). At the mouth of this creek, on the south side of the Yukon River, a new town has been laid out and named "Rampart City." At the time of our arrival the city consisted of a good log store building, two or three log huts, and half a dozen tents. Twenty-one men were reported at work in the mines along the creek, about 6 miles from the village. A mining district had been established, with Mr. O. C. Miller as recorder, and town lots were sold at $300 each. Nearly a month later I returned down the river. Lots had doubled in price, and the population had increased to about 200. A month later the population had increased to 1,000, and corner lots were selling at $200 and $300 in gold dust, and probably by this time it is the largest city in central Alaska. An acquaintance sank a shaft 4 feet square and 20 feet deep to bed rock, taking out $3,250 in gold nuggets.

The course of the steamer after leaving Rampart City was through the canyon, the hills rising on both sides of the river from 500 to 2,000 feet, making interesting scenery.

On July 15, at 2 o'clock a. m., we reached Fort Hamlin, a new trading post established by the Alaska Commercial Company; and soon after we passed out from the canyon into that portion of the river known as the Yukon Flats, where it broadens out into a lake-like expanse 80 miles wide, filled with many islands, no hills being visible on either side. The flats continue for over 200 miles, at the upper end being situated the mining town of Circle City. In a former period, when the Rampart Mountains stood a barrier to the drainage westward, this great plain, comprising an area of 100,000 square miles, more or less, was covered with water, into which the Porcupine, the Pelly, the White, the Stewart, the Birch, and other streams poured their floods, washing down the mountains and the hills and covering the plain many feet deep with sediment. In places where the present streams have cut a channel through this sediment heaps of driftwood were found buried in 200 feet of clay. Geological evidences show the bed of the Porcupine River 200 feet higher than now. If it is true, as reported, that the bed of a great river exists among the mountain ravines of southern Alaska, it may be that it was the outlet of this inland sea. In time, through erosion or rending of the mountain barriers by earthquake or in some other way, an outlet was opened to the westward, and the released waters swept irresistibly to the sea, carrying with their angry flood sediment which extended the land hundreds of miles into the Bering Sea. After the subsidence of the waters this region became the home of the mastodon, the bones and tusks of which are found in large numbers.

On July 16 we met and passed the steamer *J. J. Healy* on its way down the river.

Among the passengers was Professor Ogilvie, of the Canadian geological survey. Being anxious to see the old historic Fort Yukon, of the Hudson Bay Fur Company, and the mouth of the Porcupine River, in the neighborhood of which we were on the evening of the 16th, I concluded to remain up all night. At midnight (12.45 a. m.) I saw the sun rise in the north, like a great globe of bright, glowing, red-hot iron in a furnace. About 6 a. m. we passed the fort, without stopping. A large number of natives lined the banks of the river. Besides numerous tents, there were several log houses, among them being a small one surmounted by a cross and belonging to the Episcopal mission. A mile and a half east of the station we passed the site of the old Hudson Bay Fur Company's post, now abandoned. Only a clear space and a few foundations mark the place once occupied by the post. A good-sized cemetery occupies a dry mound back of the ruins, and is a touching reminder of the days when this far-off wilderness spot under the Arctic Circle was the center of life and civilization, with its loves and hates, hopes and fears, strifes and ambitions.

Here the all-powerful Hudson Bay Fur Company met and contended with the equally powerful Russian-American Fur Company, backed by their respective Governments.

Plucking the brilliant flowers of the fire plant as a souvenir for a friend in New York City, who was born here when her father ruled as the chief factor of the company, I watched the receding spot until a turn in the river hid it from sight.

As yesterday, the scenery continued through an expanse of river, widening out into a lake, filled with many islands, covered with white pine, aspen, and willows, and sand bars so recently out of the water as to be bare of all vegetation.

We had expected to be in Circle City during the night of July 18, but green firewood, swift current, low stage of water, and worn-out boiler flues all conspired to detain us, so that morning found us still 20 miles away. The morning dawned with a cold rain and great discomfort among the passengers. At 10 o'clock we stopped to take on wood. Mr. R. Wilson, who is in charge of the wood yard for steamers, at the same time provides fresh vegetables. As soon as a sufficient number of trees are cut down to let the sunlight reach the ground, he loosens the soil between the stumps and roots with a pickax and sows turnips, rutabagas, and cabbage. Last season, on a quarter of an acre of that uncleared ground between stumps, he raised and sold 3,000 pounds of turnips at 15 cents per pound, besides large quantities of cabbages and rutabagas. The rutabaga seed sown the last of May, this season, now (in less than two months) have a spread of leaves 2 feet across.

At 1 p. m. we reached Circle City. Mr. Kjellman, who had preceded me by another boat, met me at the landing; he had been able to make an overland trip to the mines tributary to the city and had ascertained that the whole region was admirably adapted for the support of reindeer and for the successful running of reindeer expresses and freight lines. Circle City is the largest collection of well-built log cabins that I have seen; at least in a great many years. Four large store and ware houses are made of corrugated galvanized iron. The opera and dance houses and two or three of the more pretentious residences are of hewn logs. The log residence of the North American Transportation and Trading Company is said to have cost $20,000, and that of Mr. Jack McQueston $15,000. The great majority of the buildings are small, one-story cabins built of logs, the spaces between the logs being filled with moss. The roofs are made with poles covered with moss, on which is placed a foot of dirt. A year ago the place had a population of 2,000; to-day there are about 50, and the majority of them are expecting to leave on our boat.

Circle City was founded in the fall of 1894, and named because of its nearness to the Arctic Circle. It is the distributing point for the rich gold placer mines of Birch Creek, which is a river 6 miles east of Circle City and runs a distance of between 200 and 300 miles in a general course parallel with the Yukon River. Among the interesting tributaries of Birch Creek is "Preachers Creek," so named because first explored by a missionary in search of fossils, which abound in some portions of the Yukon flats. Gold was first found on Birch Creek in 1893. Since then prospecting has been going on so vigorously that the creek, with its many tributaries, has been definitely proven to be very rich in mineral deposits. Although the rush this present season is to the more recently discovered mines on the Klondike River, yet 400 miners remain at work on Birch Creek, and doubtless in a year or two the now almost depopulated Circle City will be again peopled.

During last winter a successful public school was kept at this place by Miss A. Fulcomer, but in the spring, when the miners left for the Klondike, they were accompanied by their families and children and the school was broken up.

Leaving Circle City at 9 o'clock in the evening, we soon met the steamer *Alice* on her way down the river. Just above Circle City the river leaves the flats and is again bordered on both sides by abrupt hills of sand and limestone with veins of granite and crystalline gneiss, which add to the pleasure of the traveler.

During the night we passed a small Indian settlement known as "Charley's Village," 22 miles from Circle City. This community has received the gospel from the English missionaries, who have been in this region since 1858.

On the evening of July 19 the monotony of the trip was relieved by the discovery on the river bank of a moose doe and her fawn. At once arose the greatest excitement on the steamer—a score of men rushing for their rifles, and a fusilade of shots commenced, both animals being killed. The steamer was landed, and men, women, and children ran into the bushes to see the game, which was brought on board.

In the afternoon of July 20 we passed the small stern-wheel steamer, the *Koyukuk*, bound for the Klondike mines. The next morning, in trying to get at some driftwood for fuel, the steamer ran aground, where we remained until about 6 p. m., when we were again afloat.

On July 22 the steamer stopped to "wood up" opposite a remarkable headland, showing a beautiful geological formation of folded rock. Frequently during the day masses of loose rock came rumbling down the face of the cliff into the water.

At noon on the 23d we passed two remarkable rocks, known as "The Old Man" and "The Old Woman." Upon the top of one of these shaft-like rocks one of the old fort traders has requested to be buried: an appropriate resting place for the sole pioneer white man in that region. At 6.30 p. m. we were startled by the cry of "A man overboard." The accident befell one of the deck hands, who had become insane, and the untrained crew were so long getting a boat into the water that the man drowned. The body was not recovered. At 7 p. m. we passed the mouth of Coal Creek, and soon after sighted on the west shore the wrecked hull of the steamer *Arctic*. She was frozen up in the ice during the previous winter, and in order to loosen her in the ice this spring giant powder was used, with the result of blowing her bottom out. Boiler and engines were removed, to be placed in another boat. Coal Creek enters the Yukon from the east about 7 miles from Forty Mile Creek and is navigable for a few miles. It flows through a limestone formation. Extensive beds of lignite coal are reported in the neighborhood.

About 9 p. m. Fort Cudahy, at the mouth of Forty Mile Creek, was reached. Adjoining this is a trading post of the North American Transportation and Trading Company. Near by is Fort Constantine, a stockade post occupied by the Canadian mounted police, Captain Constantine in charge. On the opposite, south side of the mouth of Forty Mile Creek is the village of Forty Mile, which has grown up around the old trading station of Jack McQueston. Down Forty Mile Creek is Buxton, a Church of England mission station, which was established in 1887.

We have now reached the western limit of the wonderful missions of the Church Missionary Society of England in northwest Canada. Commenced in 1822 by the Rev. John West, who settled at a Hudson Bay fur-trading station near Lake Winnipeg, they have extended until now they embrace nearly all the Indian tribes extending from the north boundary of the United States to the Arctic Ocean and from Labrador to the Alaskan line. Through all this wide region the gospel of Christ has been preached in eleven different languages, and thousands upon thousands of Indians have felt the transforming power of His life in their works and lives. This region belongs to the diocese of Selkirk, and was created in 1890 by the division of the diocese of Mackenzie River. The Rev. Dr. W. C. Bompas, who entered the mission work in 1865 and was consecrated bishop of the diocese of Mackenzie River in 1874, in the division took the bishopric of Selkirk. The diocese of Selkirk has but three or four central stations, Rampart House, on the Porcupine River, being one of them. This station was established in 1882, but owing to the decrease of the fur trade and consequent removal of the trading store and further discovery of gold on the Yukon River, nearly all the natives have left, and it is probable that the station will be discontinued at an early day. Buxton, on the Yukon River at the mouth of Forty Mile Creek, was established in 1887. Being in the center of the newly discovered gold diggings, it is well located to reach the native population. Selkirk was located in 1892 and Dawson in 1897.

Missionaries.—Right Rev. William C. Bompas, bishop, resident at Pelly; Miss M. K. Mellet, assistant. Rev. and Mrs. H. A. Nailor and Rev. and Mrs. B. Totty, at Buxton. Rev. F. F. Flewelling, Rev. Mr. Bowen, and Mr. G. A. McLeod, at Dawson. Rev. and Mrs. J. Hanksley, Fort Yukon.

No more devoted, self-sacrificing men and women are to be found in the territories of England, Canada, and the United States, who are hid away from the world's observation in the vast solitudes of arctic and subarctic North America, toiling to bring light and joy of Christ into the darkened homes of these dwellings of the North, than these missionaries. The world never ceases to honor the names of Kane, Hays, Hall, Franklin, Kellett, Ross, Greely, Peary, Nansen, and many others, who in the cause of science spend one, two, and three years in the arctic regions; but few stop to think of and to honor the men and women who, for the sake of Christ and precious souls, are not merely traveling for a few months, but are toiling year after year amid the rigors and privations and loneliness and long months of continuous darkness of the arctic winters. Let the church be true to herself and honor such consecrated sons and daughters as Dr. and Mrs. Marsh at Point Barrow; Mr. and Mrs. Lopp at Bering Straits; Mr. and Mrs. Gambell at St. Lawrence Island; Mr. and Mrs. Brevig, of Port Clarence, the Swedish missionaries at Unalaklik and Golovin Bay; Messrs. Chapman and Prevost and their devoted wives on the Yukon River, with Bishop Bompas and his assistants in the Northwest Territory.

Forty Mile Creek is so named because it is 40 miles from the old Hudson Bay Fur Company's trading post at Fort Reliance. It is about 250 miles long and has many tributaries, all of which carry free gold, the discovery of which has attracted the attention of the world to the upper Yukon region. The Forty Mile Creek drains the mountainous region between the valleys of the Yukon and Tanana. Near Forty Mile is Miller Creek, which has proven very rich in gold. For two or three years Forty Mile and Fort Cudahy were typical mining towns, with saloons and gambling and dance halls in abundance. In 1894 rich discoveries were made on Birch Creek, and Forty Mile was deserted for Circle City, which after two and a half years of fevered existence has been in turn deserted for the new mines on the Klondike. While the mines tributary to Fort Cudahy and Forty Mile are on the American side, the villages themselves are on the Canadian side of the international boundary line.

Wishing to visit the Church of England missions at Buxton, on Saturday, July 24, I made two attempts to cross Forty Mile Creek in a rowboat, but was unable to accomplish it, owing to the strong current. At Fort Cudahy I found in connection with the North American Transportation and Trading Company's station an excellent garden, in which were growing peas, beans, lettuce, turnips, rutabagas, beets, potatoes, celery, and parsnips.

About 5 p. m. the steamer swung out from her landing for Dawson, which place we reached the following morning, July 25, at 6 o'clock. Nearly the entire population seemed to be at the landing, either to greet friends or from curiosity to witness the landing of newcomers. Capt. John J. Healy, manager of the North American Trading and Transportation Company, was on hand to extend to me the hospitality of his home during my stay. Although it was Sunday, the two sawmills were running day and night; every kind of business, especially house building, was in full blast. Four thousand people were living in tents, and an arctic winter approaching.

The temperature for January, 1896, was 47½° below zero. during the winter the lowest point being 77° below zero. Dawson is 50 miles from Fort Cudahy, on the north of the Yukon and southwest bank of the Klondike River. It is 6 miles above the site of the old Hudson Bay Fur Company's post of Fort Reliance. The town is situated in an undrained swamp, and much sickness prevails among the population. The city is about eight months old and is regularly laid out in streets and squares. Lots fronting on the river are selling for $7,000 cash in gold; back of the stream, from $1,000 to $3,000. Lumber is $150 per thousand feet at the mill and $300 a thousand when it reaches the mines. Some of the early lumber sawed by hand cost the miners at the rate of $750 per thousand feet. Salmon and moose were $50 per pound; hay, $125 per ton, and none to be had; wages, $10 to $12 per day, with mechanics at $15; ice, $1 per pound; flour at $12 per hundredweight; a team of horses and driver, $50 per day. The Canadian Government was erecting comfortable headquarters for the mounted police, and large log warehouses were in process of construction for the two commercial companies. The banks of the river were lined with scows and flatboats, in which the population had floated down the river; others of these boats had been covered with canvas and turned into houses. At half past 2 in the afternoon Rev. Mr. Bowen, of the Church of England, held a service, which I missed, not having been able to ascertain the hour at which it was to be held.

The mines are from 12 to 25 miles up the Klondike River from Dawson. The claims are 300 or 400 feet wide up and down the stream and across the flats. These claims were being held at $100,000 to $1,000,000 each. Quarter interests in these claims were selling at $50,000 each. The claims on the Klondike and its tributaries were all taken up long before my arrival, and weeks before the tidings of their value reached the distant world. Would-be miners, however, can find in the valleys of the Stewart, Pelly, and other streams of the Northwest Territory, in the valley of the Yukon and all its tributaries and their innumerable creeks and brooks gold fields of greater or less richness; indeed, the area of the gold field practically covers four-fifths of the entire area of Alaska, and will furnish claims for many years to come. The newcomer usually pitches a tent, and, when he secures employment or a claim, erects a small one-story log cabin for shelter. Moss is filled in between the logs, and in winter snow is piled up over the house, making it very comfortable. Ice is usually melted in winter for drinking water, or cakes of ice are drawn to the house and piled outside of the door to be brought in, as occasion demands, and melted into water.

At 7 o'clock p. m., July 26, having bid adieu to friends and acquaintances at Dawson City, our steamer swung loose from the landing and was soon racing down the river with a swift current, reaching Fort Cudahy at 10 o'clock, having made in three hours down stream a distance that required fourteen hours to make on the way up.

The following day we reached Circle City, having traveled in twenty-four hours what took us seven days to go up, but our hopes were soon to be blighted. Shortly after leaving Circle City our steamer was caught by the current and swung upon a sand bar, where we lay nineteen days.

On the 13th of August, about 1 p. m., the cry of "Steamboat!" was heard, and soon after the *J. J. Healy* was made out on her return down the river, and at 6 p. m., after our detention of nineteen days, the passengers were transferred from the *Weare* to the *Healy*, upon which we continued our journey to St. Michael.

On the evening of August 20 the steamer *Hamilton* was met coming up the river. Being the first steamer to carry a search-light, it created much interest and some consternation among the natives. The two steamers were tied up together for the night. On the incoming steamer was the first rush of miners that had been able to start from the outside after the tidings had reached them. It was crowded with gold seekers and adventurers, among them being ex-Governor McGraw, of the State of Washington; also many special correspondents of newspapers, including the New York World and Herald, the San Francisco Chronicle, Examiner, and Call; also the Post-Intelligencer and other Seattle papers. A supply of papers was secured and greatly appreciated after being over two months without any news from the outside world.

On the 30th of August the revenue cutter *Bear* reached St. Michael, and through the courtesy of Captain Tuttle I was permitted to move my headquarters to that ship. On the 16th we sailed for a visit to Teller Reindeer Station, Cape Prince of Wales, and the new purchase station at St. Lawrence Bay, reaching Teller Reindeer Station September 18. An inspection of the station was made. Four families of Lapp herders and teachers whose time had expired were taken on board the *Bear* for transportation to Puget Sound en route to their homes in Lapland. Five young Eskimo girls and one boy were also received on board for transportation to Puget Sound on their way to the Indian school at Carlisle, Pa. On the morning of the 20th the ship sailed for St. Lawrence Bay, Siberia, reaching there on the morning of the 21st. Mr. John W. Kelly, in charge of the station, and his assistants (Messrs. Siem and St. Leger) were found in good health. The new building was about completed, and 200 head of deer had already been secured toward the herd which is to be transported to Alaska next season. Sailing the same evening and making a short call at King Island, St. Michael was reached on the 23d. Changing my quarters from the cutter *Bear* to the cutter *Corwin*, I was given a passage by Captain Herring to San Francisco. On September 26 the *Corwin* made a landing at St. Lawrence Island, and the captain very kindly took on board the teachers, Mr. and Mrs. V. C. Gambell, Mrs. Gambell needing to return to the States on account of ill health. On the 30th we reached Dutch Harbor, where a stay of two or three days was made for coaling ship. Sailing from Dutch Harbor October 3, we reached San Francisco on the 13th and Washington November 1, thus completing a trip of 21,736 miles.

There are two general ways of reaching the mines in the Yukon and Klondike. The way involving the least hardship is by the ocean and from the Pacific coast to St. Michael by ocean steamer, from thence up the Yukon River by river steamer to the mines.

EDUCATION IN ALASKA.

Distances from St. Michael up the Yukon River.

	Miles.		Miles.
From San Francisco to Unalaska	2,369	Manork Creek	1,075
From Unalaska to St. Michael	800	Stevens Houses	1,144
St. Michael to Pastolik (mouth of Yukon)	72	One Eyes	1,279
Kcotalek	77	Mouth of Porcupine	1,344
Kcesilvak	154	Fort Yukon	1,353
" Foot of the Mountain "	193	Sonate Village	1,386
Audreafski	216	Circle City	1,394
Russian mission	315	Charley River	1,456
Holy Cross Mission	410	Seventy Mile Creek	1,516
Anvik	457	Ogilvie's Camp Boundary Line	1,560
Nulato	648	Square Rock	1,584
Kokrinos	800	Fort Cudahy	1,596
Burning Mountain	849	Forty Mile Creek	1,598
Tozamakat	883	Fort Reliance	1,640
Mouth of Tanana	897	Dawson	1,650
Rampart Rapids	1,034	Klondike	1,652

The following stern-wheel steamers were running on the river this summer: Belonging to the North American Trading and Transportation Company were the *P. B. Weare*, *J. J. Healy*, and *C. H. Hamilton*; belonging to the Alaska Commercial Company were the *Alice*, *Yukon*, a barge *Marguerite*, the steam launch *Beaver*, and *New Racket*, owned by A. Harper; the *Koukuk*, by G. C. Bettles; the *St. Michael*, by the Roman Catholic mission; the *Northern Light*, by the American Episcopal mission, and the *Explore*, by the Russian Catholic mission. The fare from Seattle to Juneau during the summer ranges from $150 to $300 per passenger. The drawback to this route consists in the fact that the miner does not reach the mines until the short arctic summer is half gone. The harbor at St. Michael does not open until from the middle of June to the middle of July, and it is impossible for ocean vessels to reach St. Michael on account of the ice before the middle of June at the earliest, and from the 1st of July to the 1st of August to the mines, according to the ice conditions on the coast. The more difficult and popular route is that by way of southeast Alaska; a comfortable vessel from Puget Sound to the northern end of Lynn Canal or Chilkoot Inlet, or an ocean steamer to Dyea and Skagway, rival towns 6 miles apart on the head waters of Chilkoot Inlet in southeastern Alaska.

Those starting from Skagway take what is known as the White Pass, and those from Dyea the Chilkoot Pass. With the present conditions of those passes, the Chilkoot Pass is probably the preferable, but both of them require the undergoing of considerable hardship. The Chilkoot and White passes involve some 30 or 40 miles' climb from the mountains on foot, which brings one to the lakes at the head waters of the Yukon River, where boats, barges, and rafts are constructed upon which the traveler floats down to the mines. To the westward of the Chilkoot Pass is what is known as the Dalton Trail. This pass crosses the mountains at a much lower elevation than either of the others and involves a trip on foot or horseback of 250 miles. This is the trail used for driving over to the Yukon River beef, cattle, and sheep. It is to the eastward of Chilkoot Pass, commencing either at Fort Wrangell and ascending the Stikine River to Telegraph Creek, thence overland by way of Lake Teslin, or starting from Juneau and going by the Taku Inlet and River to Lake Teslin, and passing down the waters of the same to the Yukon. At present neither of these routes is sufficiently open to make them feasible, as a number of miners found to their great loss during the past summer. The distances by the Chilkoot Pass route are as follows:

Distances from Dyea.

	Miles.		Miles.
From Seattle to Dyea	1,060	Hootalinqua River	216
From Dyea to the head of canoe navigation	6	Cassiar Bar	242
		Big Salmon River	249
To the summit of the Chilkoot Pass	14	Little Salmon River	285
Head of Lake Lindeman	23	Five Fingers Rapids	344
Foot of Lake Lindeman	27	Rink Rapids	350
Head of Lake Bennett	28	Pelly River	403
Foot of Lake Bennett	53	White River	499
Caribou Crossing	56	Stewart River	509
Foot of Tagish Lake	73	Sixty Mile Post	529
Head of Lake Marsh	78	Klondike	578
Foot of Lake Marsh	97	Fort Reliance	582
Head of canyon	123	Forty Mile Post	628
Foot of canyon	124	Fort Cudahy	628
Head of White Horse Rapids	125	Circle City	798
Tahkeona River	140	Fort Yukon	839
Head of Lake Le Barge	156	Rampart City	1,119
Foot of Lake Le Barge	184		

Prices at Dawson, Yukon, spring of 1897.

Articles.	Price.	Articles.	Price.
1 cup of coffee and 1 lump sugar	$0.50	Hudson Bay blanket	$30.00
1 meal (restaurant)	1.50	Blue overalls	2.50
Shaving	1.00	Smoking tobacco......per pound	2.00
Hair cut	1.50	Chewing tobacco............do	2.00
Washing calico dress	1.00	Ham...........................do	.65
Washing 1 garment (apron, no starch)	.50	Alum..................per ounce	.50
Eggs...................per dozen	4.50-5.00	Butter..................per pound	.50-.60
Fresh eggs ....each	1.00	Candles................per dozen	1.00
Whisky................per gallon	25.00-34.00	Scott's Emulsion.........per pint	3.00
Flour.............per 100 pounds	12.00	Salts..................per ounce	.25
Condensed milk..........per can	.50	Coal oil..............per gallon	1.25
Potatoes..............per pound	.20	Sarsaparilla...........per quart	3.00
Canned vegetables	.75	Hostetter's Bitters	3.00
Canned fruits	.75	Castor oil............per ounce	.25
Canned cherries	1.00	Cough mixture............do	1.00
Cheese..............per pound	1.00	Pond's Extract.........per pint	3.00
Pickles.............quart bottle	2.75	Glycerin..............per ounce	.50
Sugar:		Small sheet-iron camping stove	35.00
Granulated........per pound	.25	Royal baking powder	1.00
C........................do	.20	Pepper (2 ounces)	.25
Matches..............per bunch	.25	Rice..................per pound	.20
Extracts...........½-pint bottle	1.00	Nutmegs.................do	4.00
Bass ale................do	2.00	Dried fruits.............do	.25
Tea:		Dried tongue	.75
Poor grade.........per pound	1.00	Washboard	2.50
Better..................do	1.25	Common broom	1.50
Bacon..................do	.50	Washtub (galvanized iron)	4.00-5.00
Vinegar............per quart	1.00	Common laundry soap....6 bars	1.00
Gum boots, hip	12.00	Clothespins...........per dozen	.25
Beans.............per pound	.15	Thread..................spool	.25
		Needles.................package	.25

RELIEF FOR SUFFERING MINERS.

During the summer just passed the water in the Yukon River reached a very low stage, preventing the usual steamer transportation along the mining towns on the upper courses of that river. Large quantities of provisions were landed by the ocean steamers at St. Michael, but owing to the inability of the river steamers to ascend the river these supplies could not be distributed to the points where they were needed; consequently as the close of navigation approached it was found that the miners were facing the long arctic winter without sufficient supplies of food. The destitution was so great that a call was made upon the Government to organize relief. Many plans were suggested to the Government. After weighing these plans it was found that the only possible solution was to take the reindeer trained to harness that were in the neighborhood of St. Michael and with them freight provisions to the settlements on the Yukon. Hence on the 22d of September you sent to William A. Kjellmann, superintendent of the Government herds in Alaska, the following telegram:

"By direction of the Secretary of the Interior, Mr. Kjellmann will assemble at once all of the available reindeer trained for harness, teamsters, and sleds, and report at St. Michael to Colonel Randall to transport supplies to Dawson City if necessary. Obtain all deer trained to harness that can be spared from Cape Prince of Wales, Golovin Bay, and Cape Nome, together with apprentices trained as teamsters and willing to go. Promise wages to all teamsters. Deer borrowed from other stations will be replaced. Also consult the United States commissioner at St. Michael.

"W. T. HARRIS, *Commissioner.*"

Upon receiving the dispatch, which was carried by way of ship to St. Michael, Mr. Kjellmann at once secured a boat and crew of Eskimos. which he sent with a copy of the dispatch to Dr. A. N. Kittilsen, in charge at the Teller Reindeer Station. Dr. Kittilsen was directed to drive the herd as soon as possible to the new station established on the Unalaklik River, and upon his arrival there placed himself in communication with Lieut. Col. G. M. Randall, U. S. A., commanding United States military post at St. Michael. Mr. Kjellmann also ordered the building of a sufficient number of sleds, to be ready upon the arrival of the deer trained to harness. These deer, operated by the War Department from St. Michael, will be able to relieve the destitution as far up the river as Rampart City (1,075 miles from St. Michael by the mouth of the river).

These arrangements were no sooner consummated than tidings came from the Arctic coast of Alaska that eight whaling vessels, carrying crews aggregating about 400 men, had been unexpectedly caught in the ice and the men were in danger of starvation. Many plans were proposed for a relief expedition, but, as in the former case, it was found that no plan was practicable that was not based upon the use of the reindeer. Accordingly the Government, on the 16th of November, issued orders for the revenue cutter *Bear* to proceed north until stopped by ice, then to make a determined effort to send Lieut. D. H. Jarvis and two or three men over the ice to the mainland. Having effected a landing, the party are to proceed to Cape Prince of Wales, secure the services of W. T. Lopp, a Congregational missionary, borrow his reindeer herd and also the herd belonging to a native Eskimo by the name of Antisarlook, and with these two herds proceed overland 500 or 600 miles in December and January to Point Barrow, or until the whalers are found and relief afforded.

As the season advanced the accounts of the shortage of food in the Yukon Valley became more and more alarming, and on the 18th of December Congress voted to be expended, under the direction of the Secretary of the Interior, the sum of $200,000, to be used for the taking of relief into the region of the Upper Yukon Valley. As the reindeer in the neighborhood of St. Michael can not be reached at this season of the year on account of ice, and fresh importations can not be made from Siberia on the same account, it is planned to send to Lapland, procure from 500 to 600 reindeer trained to harness and 50 or 60 experienced drivers, transport them across the Atlantic to New York, thence across the continent to Seattle, and from Seattle to Dyea, near the Chilkoot Pass in southeast Alaska. At this point arrangements will be made by means of these trained deer to carry provisions to the mining camps in the Upper Yukon Valley.

Thus when an exigency arose in which hundreds of men were threatened with starvation it was found that the reindeer furnished the only reasonable plan for the relief of the miners. The reindeer are a necessity for the development of the new mines and the supply of sufficient food for the miners. The more rapidly domestic reindeer can be introduced into that country the more rapidly new sections can be visited and developed.

In conclusion, I desire to acknowledge the many courtesies received from the honorable Secretary of the Treasury; Capt. C. F. Shoemaker, chief of Revenue-Cutter Service; Capt. Francis Tuttle, commanding cutter *Bear;* Capt. W. J. Herring, commanding the *Corwin*, together with officers and crews of both vessels; also the North American Commercial Company, their agents in Alaska, and Capt. J. C. Barr, commanding the river steamer *J. J. Kelly*, and Captain Kidtlson, commanding the steamer *Portland.*

Expenditure of reindeer fund.

Year.	Annual appropriation.	Station supplies. a	Barter goods. bc	Salaries of reindeer teachers.	Freight	Traveling expenses.	Printing.	Incidentals.	Coal for U.S. revenue cutter Bear.	Total expended.	Balance.
1894	$6,000	$2,284.15	$2,473.41	$540.58					$700.00	$5,998.14	$1.86
1895	7,500	3,811.83	1,767.26	683.80			$150.00		1,081.50	7,494.39	5.61
1896	7,500	3,177.62	1,348.43		$1,450.71	$100.00	236.84	$127.50	1,050.00	7,491.10	8.90
1897	12,000	4,065.28	2,610.54	2,982.20	1,738.50	200.00	267.22	5.10		11,868.84	131:16
Total	33,000	13,338.88	8,199.64	4,206.58	3,189.21	300.00	654.06	132.60	2,831.50	32,852.47	147.53

Value station property, barter goods, and supplies on hand June 30, 1897...... 6,817.49

Total cost of reindeer in Alaska to June 30, 1897...... 26,034.98

Cost per head of 1,295 reindeer ...... d 20.10

a Supplies at station consist of provisions for herders, material for herders' clothing, coal, lumber, hardware, furniture, tools, guns, ammunition, boats, tents, medicines, surgical implements, medical books.
b Barter goods in stock at Teller Reindeer Station were transferred to new reindeer purchasing station at St. Lawrence Bay, Siberia, August, 1897.
c In all traffic in the arctic region barter goods are used in lieu of money. Money is useful only where there are markets and shops with stores of goods on sale. Neither Russian money nor the money of any other nations is used among the tribes in northeastern Siberia, nor on the Alaskan coasts opposite.
d This does not include the cost of the 171 reindeer bought with barter goods purchased with the fund of $2,156 contributed by benevolent individuals in 1893.

Number and distribution of domestic reindeer in Alaska June 30, 1897.

Location of herds.	Old deer.	Fawns.	Total.
Government herd, Teller Station, Port Clarence	343	126	469
Cape Nome herd, in charge of native Charlie	193	85	278
Golovin Bay herd (Swedish mission)	70	40	110
Golovin Bay herd (for Episcopal mission)	69	40	109
Cape Prince of Wales herd (Congregational mission)	243	124	367
Tavotuk, apprentice at Teller Station	15	11	26
Sekeogluk, apprentice at Teller Station	7	5	12
Wocksock, apprentice at Teller Station	4	2	6
Ahlook, apprentice at Teller Station	3	2	5
Electoona, apprentice at Teller Station	4	3	7
Moses, apprentice at Golovin Bay	20	11	31
Martin, apprentice at Golovin Bay	12	7	19
Okitkon, apprentice at Golovin Bay	10	5	15
Tatpan, apprentice at Golovin Bay	7	5	12
Total	1,000	466	1,466

Increase from 1892 to 1897.

	1892.	1893.	1894.	1895.	1896.	1897.
Total from previous year		143	323	492	743	1,000
Fawns surviving		79	145	276	357	466
Purchased during summer	171	124	120	123		
Total, October 1	171	346	588	891	1,100	1,466
Loss	28	23	96	148	100	
Carried forward	143	323	492	743	1,000	

Number of reindeer that have been lent by the Government to missionary societies and natives, the Government reserving the right after a term of not less than three years to call upon the mission station or individual for the same number of deer as composed the herd loaned:

```
                                                                        Deer.
August, 1894, to the Congregational Missionary Society's Station at Cape Prince of Wales.  118
February, 1895, to Eskimo Charlie and 3 native assistants.................................  112
January 16, 1896, to the Swedish Mission Station at Golovin Bay...........................   50
January 16, 1896, to the St. James Episcopal Mission Station, Yukon River.................   50
    Total................................................................................  330
```

WITHDRAWN FOR RELIEF EXPEDITIONS.

October, 1897, withdrawn from the Government herd at Teller Station and from the herds at Golovin Bay from 100 to 200 deer trained to harness for use, if necessary, in drawing food from St. Michael to Dawson, under directions of Lieutenant-Colonel Randall at St. Michael.

December, 1897, for the relief of the whalers in the Arctic Sea, the Cape Nome herd, numbering 278, and the Cape Prince of Wales herd, numbering 367, to be under the direction of Lieut. D. H. Jarvis, U. S. revenue cutter *Bear*, promising to make good those borrowed by a transfer from the Government herd during the summer of 1898.

I have the honor to be, sir, very respectfully, your obedient servant,

SHELDON JACKSON.

Hon. W. T. HARRIS, LL. D.,
 Commissioner of Education, Washington, D. C.

www.ingramcontent.com/pod-product-compliance
Lightning Source LLC
Chambersburg PA
CBHW031608110426
42742CB00037B/1327